For my father, who first taught me to dream,
My mother, for encouraging those dreams,
And Michael, for making my dreams come true.
*(Shut the door)*

# Dated Jekyll Married Hyde

## Or, Whatever Happened to Prince Charming?

**Laura Jensen Walker**

**SPIRE**

Published by Fleming H. Revell
a division of Baker Book House Company
P.O. Box 6287, Grand Rapids, MI 49516-6287
www.bakerbooks.com

Spire edition published 2003

Previously published by Bethany House Publishers under the title *Dated Jekyll, Married Hyde*

Printed in the United States of America

0-8007-8710-2

## Books by Laura Jensen Walker

*Dated Jekyll, Married Hyde*
*Love Handles for the Romantically Impaired*
*Mentalpause*
*Thanks for the Mammogram!*
*Through the Rocky Road and into the Rainbow Sherbet*

**Laura Jensen Walker** is a popular speaker, author, and former newspaper columnist. Her books include *Love Handles for the Romantically Impaired*, *Through the Rocky Road and into the Rainbow Sherbet*, *Mentalpause*, and *Thanks for the Mammogram!* She lives in Northern California with her Renaissance-man husband, Michael.

# Acknowledgments

John Donne said, "No man is an island, entire of itself. Every man is a piece of the continent, a part of the main." Thanks to the following for being a "part of" my first book:

To my husband and best friend, Michael, who served as sounding board, anecdote approver, editor, and No. 1 cheerleader—thanks for letting me share so much of our marriage with so many people, honey. Your unwavering love is truly the wind beneath my wings. (And I think you're pretty cute, too.)

I owe a special debt of gratitude to my poet friend Katie Young, for reading all those late night and early morning faxes and for always laughing in the right places. "Girlfriend," your encouraging spirit is an incredible blessing.

To the Young family of Sebastopol—thanks for letting me steal away to your home for some much needed writing time, as well as some great cooking! (Julia, thanks for giving up your room.)

A very special thank-you to all the couples who helped either in the brainstorming process, or who graciously allowed me to use humorous anecdotes from their marriages:

Hank and Lisa Brys, Bill and Andrea Cuthbertson, Mike and Jan Duncan, Jim and Sheri Jameson, Bill and Mary Kuyper, Alan and Dana Loucks, Pat and Ken McLatchey, Diane and Warren Melick, Doug and Michelle Skinner, Bob and Shelley "K" Steed, Lana and Michael Yarbrough, Mark and Katie Young.

Thanks also to those who lent their technical expertise (and/or equipment) at critical times: Randy and Carol Allen, Curt and Peggy Clark, Joshua Cook, Mort and Bettie Eichenberg.

To my family—both my side and Michael's—thank you for your unfailing support as you watched this dream come true. (With an especially heartfelt thanks to you, Mom!)

To Lisa Cook, Lana Yarbrough, and Maria Vidos Hunt—thanks for sharing in the excitement and for your unconditional love.

To Pat and Ken McLatchey—thanks for the impromptu marital guidance and for always being there throughout our twenty-year friendship.

But above all, thank you, Lord, for fulfilling a lifelong dream that you placed in my heart as a child. You truly give us the desires of our hearts (Psalm 37:4).

# Contents

Introduction ...................................... 15

1. Dated Jekyll, Married Hyde ................... 19
   *Who is this masked (wo)man I married? You sure weren't
   like this when we were dating! (Idiosyncrasies you don't
   find out about until after you say, "I do.")*

2. Sleeping Habits of a Highly Defective Couple ........ 27
   *(or what happens when a cheerful morning person marries
   a not-so-cheerful-in-the-morning person)*

3. In Sickness and In Health ....................... 33
   *Men have the corner on the whining market when they're
   sick. "Get over it!" we long to say (and sometimes do). But
   those marriage vows before the Lord are sure welcome when
   an unexpected health crisis hits.*

4. Directionally Impaired ........................... 41
   *He says, "Turn north." She says, "Left or right?" Many
   women suffer from this directional disability, which men
   just can't seem to understand. "Just imagine a map in your
   head," they say. Right....*

5. "Where's my (fill-in-the-blank)?" ................... 49
   *Although men may know which way they're going, they
   don't know where they left their keys, wallet, and a host of
   other items. "Just remember where you last had it," we say.
   Right....*

6. Calgon vs. Soap-on-a-Rope ........................ 57
   *He prefers steaming hot showers and soap-on-a-rope while she likes to let Calgon bath salts "take her away" (for at least an hour).*

7. Shut the Door .................................... 65
   *(a misunderstanding behind closed doors)*

8. I Like Liver Paté, He Likes SpaghettiOs (Cold!) ....... 73
   *Dissecting the eating habits of the male and the female of the species.*

9. His Junk, My Treasures ........................... 79
   *Also known as, "Love me, Love my stuff." Or how women learn to cope with GI Joe collections and Elvis paintings on black velvet. (That's what spare rooms are for.)*

10. Nightmare on Our Street ........................ 87
    *Or as many refer to it, "first-house frenzy." "What do you mean we can't remodel that ugly '60s kitchen and bathroom in one week?"*

11. "Chick" Logic ................................... 95
    *(a.k.a. Laura-Logic in our household) Although she received high marks in school, she was absent the day they taught logic. For instance, she thinks moving to Seattle would be fun, but he says it rains too much. "So we'll live in the suburbs!"*

12. I Want the Moon, but He Has to Hang It ........... 103
    *She wants a new patio, but while he's laying the bricks, she's lying in the pool. (Often she comes up with the great home improvement ideas, but he gets stuck swinging the hammer.)*

13. The Nagging Gene ............................... 111
    *Many women possess it but don't realize it until they're married. Although we all vowed that we would never nag, it's hard to fight genetics.*

14. The Testosterone Tango ......................... 119
*She can two-step, chew bubble gum, rearrange the living-room furniture, and carry on a nonstop conversation all at the same time. But when he's dancing the tango, he's just doing the tango. It's gotta be a testosterone thing that makes men so single-task focused.*

15. She's Felix, He's Oscar ......................... 125
*When it comes to neatness, they're definitely "The Odd Couple." (But let's not be sexist. In some households, she's Oscar!)*

16. Sub-Mission Impossible ......................... 131
*I'm having a teensy-weensy problem with this submit stuff. After all, I'm the woman who kept a plaque on her desk in her B.C. (before Christ) days that proudly read: A WOMAN WITHOUT A MAN IS LIKE A FISH WITHOUT A BICYCLE.*

17. I Say Exquisite, He Says Cool .................... 139
*and other male/female vocabulary variations*

18. She Wants It Special Delivery, not FAXED .......... 145
*Although we like hearing the quick and basic "I Love You" from his lips, we also want sweet nothings sent "Special D."*

19. The Night He Saw Red ......................... 153
*To him, the color red means "charge." To her, it's just what she happened to wear to bed (and other bedroom misunderstandings).*

20. The In-Law Shuffle ............................. 159
*You don't just marry each other, you also marry the in-laws. And to try to keep them happy, every year finds you dashing through the snow from house-to-house at Christmas.*

21. Talk Marathons vs. the Sixty-Second Speech Sprint ... 167
*She can sit and visit for hours with family and friends, but after too much sitting, he starts to fidget or fall asleep.*

22. Hold me, Touch me, Listen to Me! .................. 175
    *When a woman is pouring out her heart to her husband,*
    *she gets a little miffed when he glances at the TV to check*
    *out* Star Trek.

23. Women Need Other Women, Men Just Need
    Their Wives ...................................... 181
    *The last male bonding thing he did was when he and his buddies went*
    *to see* Terminator 2 *for his bachelor party . . . more than five years*
    *ago. He's content to simply "connect" with his wife, while she goes*
    *into withdrawal if she goes more than a week without relating to her*
    *women friends!*

24. And They Lived Happily Ever After. . . . .......... 187
    *The couple that laughs together stays together.*

# Introduction

"God, the best maker of all marriages,
Combine your hearts in one."

—William Shakespeare

Whenever I told people I was writing a humorous book on marriage titled *Dated Jekyll, Married Hyde*, most laughed in immediate recognition and familiarity. But a few looked at me sympathetically and murmured words of comfort in an effort to console me for having found myself married to a monster.

However, their words of comfort quickly turned to raised eyebrows and a remembrance of a pressing errand when I'd explain, "But *I'm* the Hyde in our marriage!"

Not that I'm a monster, either (except for those very occasional times when my hormones take over and turn my normally sweet-natured Snow-White personality into an angry witch with a bad apple and an attitude).

I'm just not exactly the same person my husband was engaged to.

But let's be honest. Who is?

It's not that any of us—husbands or wives—deliberately set out to deceive our happily-ever-after intendeds, it's just that until we're married, we don't see all the different sides of each other.

And let's face it: we *are* different.

But the Lord made us that way. And since God doesn't make mistakes, I believe that He wants us to enjoy those differences—even delight in them.

Granted, sometimes those differences just make us want

to scream (been there, done that). In fact, I read somewhere that Ruth Bell Graham, wife of the beloved Billy Graham, was once asked if she'd ever considered divorce.

Her answer? "Divorce, no. Murder, yes."

But before you grab that baseball bat, why not do something completely silly and unexpected instead?

Personally, I like to make up goofy songs and sing them to my surprised spouse. Or, when my creative juices aren't freely flowing, I just substitute my peacock impression instead. It's loud but effective.

My husband, on the other hand, does a to-die-for Elmer Fudd impression that leaves me in stitches every time.

It's hard to fight when you're laughing together.

This is not a heavy "how-to" book with deep, psychological insights into our differences. It's simply a light-hearted romp written in hopes of bringing a smile to your face as you spot yourself (or your mate) in some of these stories.

And the next time your Jekyll/Hyde spouse does something that's irritating, remember these stories and have a good chuckle.

Unless, of course, he forgets to put the toilet seat down. Then you can just deck him.

*Marriage should be honored by all.*

—*Hebrews 13:4*

# 1

# Dated Jekyll, Married Hyde

Who *is* this masked (wo)man I married? You sure weren't like this when we were dating! (Idiosyncrasies you don't find out about until after you say, "I do.")

"Would you *let* me woo you?" my brand-new husband snapped at me on the fourth day of our marriage.

I looked up in surprise from the pile of wedding gifts I was sorting through. After all, we'd already spent a few blissful days at a charming bed-and-breakfast at the start of our week-long honeymoon. But now we were home in our tiny one-bedroom apartment, and I was eager to get settled and put everything in its place.

Michael was eager for the honeymoon to continue.

After all, he was a newlywed with just two more days left of his vacation before he had to return to work and the "real world."

Me too.

Except that I didn't want the work week to start with my new home in disarray. To me—the formerly dyed-in-the-wool romantic—it was important to get organized so that we'd return to an orderly home where we could relax at the end of a hard day. I couldn't relax in a room full of wrapping paper and discarded boxes.

Michael didn't understand. During our dating days, I couldn't get enough romance. Now here I was on our honeymoon preferring cleaning to an impromptu picnic he'd planned!

That was the first inkling he had that he'd dated Jekyll, married Hyde.

Camping was the next.

While we were dating, I'd regaled Michael with stories of rafting excursions, hikes, and camping trips from the days when I was in the singles leadership group at church. This led him to believe that I was at least a tiny bit outdoorsy. But what I had neglected to tell him was my motive behind all those outdoor excursions: a man.

I'd had a crush on one guy for years who never saw me as anything more than a friend and sister in Christ. But I was so besotted with this hiking and backpacking man that I did anything I could just to be near him. Even camp.

So poor Michael thinks he's marrying this exciting, adventurous woman who will hike and camp and spend countless hours in the great outdoors with him.

What he didn't know is that I am a slug.

Not that I have anything against spending time outside. In fact, there's nothing quite like the wind in my hair as I'm reading. Or the sound of chirping birds mingling with the sound of turning pages.

Whereas Michael had something a little more active in mind.

Our first camping trip took place two months after we were married. We went to the ocean with a large mixed group of singles and couples. Realizing by now that camping wasn't high on my list of fun things to do, Michael did everything he could to make it a pleasant experience. Starting with the monster tent he bought.

Everyone else had either a one-man pup tent or one of those two-person dome-style jobbies. Ours was a condominium in comparison. Large and luxurious, Michael thought that even I could be happy in a tent like this.

I helped him set up our deluxe outdoor accommodations, then went to visit with some friends around the camp-fire. Half an hour later, Michael joined us. But after just a few minutes of polite conversation, he nudged me and said it was getting late.

He ushered me up the hill to our condo tent and un-zipped the entrance with a flourish. Inside, the lantern, al-though turned down low, cast just enough light to illumi-nate the double-wide sleeping bag invitingly turned down atop the pumped-up air mattress.

To Michael, sleeping in a tent in the great outdoors was a romantic haven. However, I didn't find it particularly ro-mantic when I woke up freezing the next morning with sand embedded in my skin and desperately needing to go to the bathroom—a mere half mile away.

As far as I was concerned, I didn't care if I ever saw the inside of a tent again. But because I'm a supportive, loving wife who wants to make her husband happy by camping one weekend a year—when the temperature is just right, not too cold and not too hot—we load up the car and head to one of California's beautiful campgrounds. (I just make sure to pack plenty of insect repellent, extra socks, and a bagful of books.)

Michael's not the only one who dated Jekyll, married Hyde.

One of my girlfriends said that when she and her hus-band were dating, they snuggled on the couch to watch a football game together. He thought it was because she en-joyed the game.

Not exactly.

"It was because I wanted to snuggle, not because I wanted to watch football," she said. Since they've been mar-ried, she hasn't watched one game. She doesn't need to.

Now she's found other avenues of snuggling.

Then there's another friend whose husband, an avid skier, had visions of them schussing down the slopes together. She likes to ski, she's just not in the same class as he is. So he decided to help out by giving her the benefit of his expertise.

She decided she'd rather learn from a professional instructor.

Only problem was the instructor was a cute, perky "snow-bunny" who paid more attention to her husband than to her.

So much for skiing.

Still another friend said that while they were dating, her husband always ran his car through a car wash before picking her up for a date. "It was always immaculate, and I was really impressed," she told me.

Since they've been wed, the car has not seen the inside of a car wash.

We all have areas of great expectations in our marriage.

Games are a biggie for Michael and me.

During our courtship, we got together often with friends for many fun-filled, fiercely competitive evenings playing board games. Yet another one of the many things my darling and I have in common.

Except that Michael expected the games to continue once we were married—with just the two of us.

Boring with a capital B. It's just not as much fun to pursue trivia *a deux*.

But then came the evening when we discovered strip *Monopoly*.

*Love is patient, love is kind. It does not envy, it does not boast, it is not proud. It is not rude, it is not self-seeking, it is not easily angered, it keeps no record of wrongs.*

—*1 Corinthians 13:4–5*

# 2

# Sleeping Habits of a Highly Defective Couple

(or what happens when a cheerful morning person marries a not-so-cheerful-in-the-morning person)

I can fall asleep anywhere.

At the dinner table, in a noisy classroom, and in front of the computer screen at work.

There was even the time in the Air Force when I fell asleep on the commode in full combat regalia (those gas masks can sure make a person feel warm and sleepy).

My husband's a little different.

He needs a bed, or something somewhat resembling one, before he can fall asleep.

He's funny that way.

And all of the conditions have to be just right before he can fall asleep at night.

He needs a dark room, no caffeine after 3:00 P.M., and complete peace and quiet (which means no late-night philosophical discussions with *moi*).

Since I've been known to fall asleep with every light in the house blazing and to drink a cup of full-strength tea five minutes before heading for bed, none of those conditions apply to me.

I've always been a read-in-bed kind of gal myself, and all my life I'd envisioned happily-ever-after bedtimes, with my husband and I snuggled in under the covers side by side—reading.

We started out that way, but Michael always got sleepy while I was still wide-awake and enthralled with my latest mystery novel. At first, he said it was okay; I could keep reading, he'd just bury his head under the pillow to block out the light.

That worked for a little while, but then he said little noises were keeping him awake, so he popped in his ear-plugs.

However, it got to the point where even that didn't help.

One night, as I was nearing the end of an incredibly sus-penseful tale, Michael yanked the pillow off his head, pulled out his ear plugs, and asked in frustration, "Do you *have* to read so loud?"

"Huh?"

I was taken aback because I knew I'd taken great care to curb any stray giggles or exclamations of astonishment so as not to disturb my sleeping handsome.

"Your page-turning is keeping me awake," Michael com-plained.

He then compared my speed-reading style to the sound of that breakfast cereal with the three elves. Only instead of *snap, crackle, pop,* he heard *zoom, crackle, whoosh* as I rap-idly turned the pages eager to get to the end.

Another major bedroom difference between Michael and me is that he is not a morning person, while I happen to be one of those people who wakes up bright-eyed and bushy-tailed ready to face the day before my feet even slide into my slippers.

Without benefit of caffeine.

Not Michael.

He's not even coherent for the first hour after he wakes up.

My honey has to fight his way through several layers of dense sleep-fog before he's among the living. Then, with the help of a twenty-minute shower and a Diet Pepsi (his "break-fast of champions"), he's *almost* ready to greet the world.

Michael's early-morning unconsciousness doesn't stop him from functioning, however.

He's been known to wake up as he's trying to hang up the telephone. That's when he realizes he's just had a conversation with someone.

A long conversation.

But he has no idea what they discussed, or worse yet, who he talked to.

And that person on the other end has no idea that Michael was asleep while they spoke.

That's because most people mumble and sound groggy when they're not fully awake. Not my husband. He's a model of articulation.

Must be his acting training kicking in.

Michael's "sleeptalking" happened to me quite often when we were first married, and I never had a clue. I'd wake up and want to talk to him about something important—like bills or social engagements or how I'm feeling about a particular misunderstanding we've had. His eyes would be open, he'd listen and respond, and even provide thoughtful, insightful comments.

So I'd start my day thinking the situation was handled.

Later, after he'd missed an important social engagement, or wanted to discuss our misunderstanding that I'd thought we'd resolved that morning, I'd realize that he'd been only "mostly" awake.

And "mostly" for him means not remembering any-thing.

I find that amazing.

He finds it amazing that I can start my day off with an

intense spiritual discussion before I've even showered or
had a cup of tea.

And that I'm also one of those disgustingly cheerful per-
sons in the mornings.

For instance, one of our favorite musicals is *Singin' in
the Rain*. There's this great, happy number that Gene Kelly,
Debbie Reynolds, and Donald O'Connor sing after staying
up all night called "Good mornin'."

Wanting to surprise my beloved one morning, I tiptoed
around making up a breakfast tray of his favorite scrambled-
eggs-and-potatoes, blueberry bagels with cream cheese,
orange juice, and coffee. I carried it down the hall to our
bedroom and paused in the doorway before bursting into
song: "Good mornin', good mor—"

Before the second "mornin'" was out of my mouth,
Michael leapt out of bed with a mighty yell and advanced
upon what he thought was an intruder, brandishing a tennis
shoe.

Startled, I shared his breakfast that morning with the
floor.

Hmmm. I'd always wondered why so many couples in
old movies had separate bedrooms. Or at least, twin beds.

We don't need to worry about that ever happening to
us, however, since we even got a double bed instead of a king
or a queen, just so we could be closer.

Except for those nights when I snore.

> *Marriage should be honored by all, and*
> *the marriage bed kept pure.*
>
> —*Hebrews 13:4*

# 3

# **In Sickness and In Health**

Men have the corner on the whining market
when they're sick. "Get over it!" we long to say
(and sometimes do). But those marriage vows
before the Lord are sure welcome when an
unexpected health crisis hits.

I married a whiner.

Whenever my husband isn't feeling well, I know it.

I've never known anyone to make such a fuss about a headache.

Or allergies.

My girlfriends tell me their husbands are the same way. They just can't cope with pain and discomfort the same way that women can.

That's why women have the babies.

And my reaction when my husband starts to whine about his splitting head or stopped-up sinuses?

Take some Tylenol.

Blow your nose.

*Deal* with it.

It's not that I'm not compassionate. After all, I always cry at telephone commercials and disease-of-the-week movies. It's just that I've never lived in such close proximity with someone who's allergic to everything from dust mites to every grass known to man.

And I must confess, I didn't have much patience with it at first. After we'd been married just a few months, I said to Michael one day in self-righteous exasperation: "You're *always* sick. I *never* get sick."

Shortly thereafter, I experienced excruciating chest pains, and Michael had to race me to the hospital emergency room. A few days after that, I had my gallbladder removed.

Then, just a couple months later, in fact, the day after our first wedding anniversary, we found out I had breast cancer.

CANCER was all I heard, and all I could think of was death.

I was only thirty-five years old, had just graduated from college, and was happily married to the man I'd been waiting for all my life.

How could this all be taken away from me?

Well, it wasn't.

All that was taken away was a breast, some lymph nodes, and later, temporarily, my hair.

Through it all—mastectomy, chemotherapy, breast reconstruction, and baldness—Michael was by my side every step of the way. Taking care of me. Being there for me. Loving me.

I never had a moment's doubt about his loving me less because I was one breast short of a matched pair. In fact, when Michael first saw my mastectomy scar, he kissed it tenderly and said, "I *love* this scar because it means I'm going to have you with me for a *long* time."

Whoa. Conviction city.

That's when I realized that perhaps I could be a *little* bit more compassionate about my husband's allergies and terrible sinus headaches.

Especially considering what he had to put up with during my months of chemotherapy.

My oncologist told us that everyone responds differently to chemo, and there was really no way of predicting how I would react. However, he said one of his patients did so well in chemo she was even able to hide the fact that she was undergoing treatments from her employer. She'd have her session late Friday afternoon, feel a bit "flu-like" over the weekend, but be back at work Monday with no one the wiser.

Mine turned out to be a little more than "flu-like."

The dictionary's definition of flu is "an acute infectious viral disease characterized by inflammation of the respiratory tract, fever, muscular pain, and intestinal irritation."

My intestines weren't irritated, they were enraged.

This was war, and my stomach was the battlefield. During the course of the chemo war, I threw up every couple hours for nine or ten days in a row after each major battle.

I also dropped thirty pounds in thirty days.

But it's not a diet plan I'd recommend.

Those were the worst days.

And nights.

You never realize how much you depend on your body, until it starts to give out on you. Chemo kills cancer cells, but it also kills healthy cells that your body needs to function.

I had to be hospitalized for every treatment because the dosage I received was so high. The night of my first injection, I slept rather fitfully and felt nauseous, but didn't throw up.

*Hooray,* I thought. *I'm going to be one of the lucky ones who doesn't get sick.* However, the next morning while my sister and nephew were visiting, I began retching horribly. In a flash, Michael was by my side with a basin and a cool cloth for my neck.

That moment marked a turning point in my sister's relationship with my husband. That's when she realized that Michael was in for the duration.

Not that it was easy for him.

In fact, he's the first to admit that he wasn't wearing a halo.

Although I didn't know it at the time, there came a day shortly after my third treatment when Michael just couldn't take any more. So he lashed out at both God and his sister in anger and frustration.

"It's not fair," he insisted. "I didn't sign up for this."

"Yes, you did," his sister Sheri gently reminded him. "I heard you. For better or worse; in sickness and in health."

Michael honored his vows then and now. Even throughout the entire reconstruction process. Or as we called it, the "build-a-breast" route (sort of like Legos, except the pieces don't snap together).

I opted for breast reconstruction because I didn't want a daily reminder of the cancer.

The construction began in the operating room immediately after my mastectomy.

The plastic surgeon inserted a "tissue expander" into my chest to stretch the remaining tissue to make room for the saline implant that would be inserted later.

The tissue expander starts out like a flat balloon.

Or whoopee cushion.

When I'd go in for my weekly expansion, my doctor would take a tiny magnet attached to a string and circle my breast area until she found the exact location of the metallic entry point beneath my skin.

Which always made me want to say, "Contact. Start your syringes."

Especially because she then filled an enormous syringe with saline and "pumped me up."

I'd been told that I'd experience "some discomfort" as

the tissue stretched and expanded, but no one told me it would feel like I had a Frisbee jammed inside my chest.

Additionally, it takes a while for everything to settle into place, so until it did, I looked like the hunchbreast of Notre Dame.

Good thing Michael's always had a soft spot in his heart for Quasimodo.

And that he's not put off by a bald wife.

For I lost every single hair on my body—including my eyebrows and eyelashes.

One day, as Michael and I passed the bathroom mirror clad only in our birthday suits, we were struck by the contrast, so we dubbed ourselves furball and cueball.

Humor helps.

The next year, on our second wedding anniversary, I fell and fractured my elbow.

We stopped celebrating anniversaries for a while after that.

> *A cord of three strands is not quickly broken.*
>
> *—Ecclesiastes 4:12*

# 4

# **Directionally Impaired**

He says, "Turn north." She says, "Left or right?" Many women suffer from this directional disability, which men just can't seem to understand. "Just imagine a map in your head," they say. Right....

When God made Eve He left out one critical piece of anatomy: the section of the brain that knows directions. But then again, in the Garden of Eden Eve really didn't need to know which way was north or south. After all, she didn't have to navigate any highways and byways. All she had to do was frolic with Adam and the animals, eat some berries, and stay away from that tree in the center of the garden.

Well, we all know the story. She messed up big time on the latter.

But did we ever stop to think that maybe, just maybe, it's because she wasn't too sure where the center of the garden was? And that possibly, just possibly, life as we know it would be entirely different if only Eve had had Adam's sense of direction?

Many—not all—of the females of our species suffer from this directional handicap.

And men just don't get it.

They tell us, "Go north on such-and-such street and then turn east when you get to such-and-such avenue."

Huh?

Just tell me whether to turn left or right. And give me well-known landmarks. Like J. C. Penney or Baskin-Robbins.

They still don't get it.

Instead, they try to be helpful by saying, "Just imagine a map in your head."

Right. . . .

I can't even use a map on my lap, much less one in my head.

I come by my directional impairment quite naturally. My mom has always been map-challenged. She freely and cheerfully admits that her sense of direction is not one of her strong suits. However, since she somehow always manages to get where she needs to go, it hasn't been too much of a hindrance for her.

My girlfriend Katie is the same way.

"My lack of direction is my opportunity to make friends wherever I go," she says, numbering a few gas station attendants and several convenience store clerks among her newfound pals.

Her husband, a cop, doesn't quite see it the same way.

But then again, he has a hard time understanding how his clever, intelligent wife who runs her own business and knows the exact price of every single item on her grocery list before she even sets foot in the store can't find her way around a town she's lived in for nearly three years.

My husband doesn't get it, either.

Granted, I'm not a numbers queen like Katie (in fact, thanks to math, I almost didn't graduate from college). However, I can spot a misspelled word at twenty paces and whip most of our friends at *Jeopardy* and *Silver Screen Trivial Pursuit*.

My particular directional impairment began in grade school.

That's when I learned that north is at the top of the compass and south is at the bottom. Naturally, I thought that meant north was always right in front of me, and, subsequently, south was always behind me.

I made it happily through my childhood years without any major traumas due to my direction deficiency. However, this handicap really began to be a bit of a problem when I got my driver's license twentysomething years ago in Phoenix, Arizona.

Now Phoenix, being "the valley of the sun," has some pretty gorgeous natural landmarks surrounding it. The only problem is, one mountain looks pretty much like another to me. So when someone would say, "Go toward South Mountain and then head east on such-and-such street," I was clueless. South Mountain/North Mountain, what's the difference? My only saving grace was when my destination was somewhere in the vicinity of Camelback Mountain. Appropriately named, *that* was a mountain even I could identify.

However, just to be on the safe side, I learned to factor in an extra half hour whenever I was driving anywhere new and unfamiliar.

After high school, I spent five years in Europe with the Air Force. And much to my family's amazement, never got lost. That's because when I was stationed in Germany, I usually traveled by train or bus. (Besides, most of the towns and villages near the base were so small that anyone could find their way around them. Even *moi*!)

And in London, they have this fantastic color-coded subway system known as "the Underground" or "the tube."

Piece of cake. Cup of tea.

It was when I returned stateside that I had difficulty adapting.

While I was overseas, my family had moved from Phoenix to Sacramento, California. (Yes, they *did* send me their forwarding address. But they also picked me up at the airport when I arrived so I wouldn't lose my way.)

Once there, the myriad of freeways in California's capital city quite boggled my mind. Particularly because they
had such similar names. There was Interstate 80, Business
80, and the "old 880." To further confuse unsuspecting
travelers, the old 880 is now the I–80 and the old I–80 is
now Business 80.

Got that? I don't. (Those freeways were obviously
named by a man.) Besides, I hadn't even been around for
the "old 880," and still don't know what that means. And
what really messes me up is when people say, "Take 80
to..." I never know if they mean I–80 or Business 80!

Sheesh! Now I'm really in trouble: having to work with
both directions and numbers.

Even my eight-year-old nephew, Joshua, knew his way
around better than I did. One day he was along when I was
trying to figure out the way to a friend's house in a part of
town I didn't know very well. This time, I knew the general
direction I needed to go but was bewildered by the variety
of freeway options to get me there.

Joshua suggested one, but I disregarded his advice.

After all, he was only eight.

But as the lights of Sacramento began to recede behind
us, he piped up from the back seat, "Aunt Laura, we're on
our way to San Francisco."

Smart-aleck little kid.

What really confuses me are those stupid road signs that
never give enough information.

I'll be approaching an interchange, and each lane will
head me toward a different city. South Lake Tahoe. Reno. San
Francisco. Well, I don't want to go to *any* of those places. I

just want to get to my best friend Lana's house in Sacramento!

Still another day I'll be in another part of town needing to get to my friend's. I know that the last time I visited, I followed the signs toward Reno, and got off two or three exits later. So I confidently aim my car toward Reno again. But now they've moved the exit.

Why can't they just install a sign that says, *Laura, this way to Lana's house?*

The good news is that my directional aptitude has improved recently thanks to my husband and our friend Randy. They've patiently explained to me that the sun sets in the west, so all I need to do is look up, find out where the sun is, and use that as my compass point.

It works pretty well. As long as it's not the lunch hour. However, once the sun sets, it's no happy ending for me.

> *In all your ways acknowledge him, and he will make your paths straight.*
>
> *—Proverbs 3:6*

# 5

# Where's My
# (fill-in-the-blank)?

Although men may know which way they're
going, they don't know where they left their
keys, wallet, and a host of other items. "Just
remember where you last had it," we say.
Right. . . .

Although men may know which way they're going, they don't know where they left their keys, wallet, and a host of other items.

"Just remember where you last had it," we say.

Right. . . .

The first time I heard of this interesting marital phenomenon was several years ago when I was still single. I was reading a magazine article about an actress in her mid-thirties who was a first-time bride. The reporter asked her how married life was, and she said, "Great," but she never knew she'd be expected to keep track of her husband's socks.

It wasn't as if she wore them, after all. Yet invariably, a few times a week her husband would plaintively ask, "Honey, have you seen my socks?"

Of course, she was a sock or two up on the rest of us, for she had the luxury of buying a swimming pool full of socks to replace the ones her husband couldn't find. But for those of us who don't live in Hollywood, there is no choice but to become the keeper of the socks.

And the keys, wallet, checkbook, daily planner . . .

And his tools.

Since I don't even know a socket wrench from a crescent wrench, I'm always surprised when my husband asks if I've seen one of the latter. Especially since the only tools I ever use are hammers and screwdrivers.

My girlfriends agree.

"Like we would even *know* where these things are," my friend Mary said. "They're *their* things. We would have nothing to do with them."

I was relieved to hear that, because it confirmed that this behavior was definitely a guy thing. For a while, I thought that perhaps my husband's losing things was a direct reflection on my embarrassing tendency to be just a little bit disorganized in some areas.

But since Mary—our own Martha Stewart—is the most organized and creative woman I've ever known, I realized that wasn't the case.

Then there's my friend Pat, another very organized woman. Her husband, Ken, is the ultimate do-it-yourselfer. And he owns every tool known to man. Not a week goes by when he isn't working on some project around the house.

But invariably, while he's working, he'll misplace one of his beloved tools.

And he's convinced that one of his sons has picked it up.

But since neither of his boys is a chip off the old block in the handyman area, he then looks to his lovely wife, who says, "What would I want with your old screwdriver?"

"Men just don't want to admit that they misplace things," says Pat from the wisdom of nearly thirty years of marriage. "His big worry is that it will get put away. You're supposed to leave it until the project's done, be it one month, two months, or whatever."

Most husbands share Ken's fear. They insist that we

move their things before they're finished with them.

But I don't see how that applies to socks. I mean, what do you *do* with socks besides wear them?

So when a wife sees a pair of socks on the floor—in the bedroom, bathroom, living room, and even (ugh) kitchen— she does what any self-respecting Mrs. Clean would do: throws them in the dirty clothes.

There's nothing quite like walking into a spic-and-span kitchen and seeing a pair of dirty socks in the middle of the newly-scrubbed floor. Naturally, we quickly pick them up and put them in the laundry.

And just as naturally, our husbands return to resume reading the paper, and their socks have disappeared.

What's not as natural is the husband's inability to put things back in the right order in the kitchen.

Take unloading the dishwasher.

Generally, I'm the one in our marriage who does that because I spend more time in the kitchen than Michael, and I know exactly where everything goes.

But now and then my thoughtful husband will help out by unloading the dishes for me. And I appreciate it. I really do. It's just that I don't understand why it's so difficult to put the glasses back in their proper place.

I group the glasses by height, color, and style. We have some tall, pale green iced tea glasses that go on the left side of the glass cupboard, followed by the shorter, clear water glasses, followed by the same-sized clear-but-ridged water glasses. And stuck behind all of these are a couple of Michael's Mickey Mouse juice glasses.

Well, when I go to reach for a water glass after Michael's unloaded the dishwasher, there's Mickey, front and center, grinning at me. Right behind him is a tall green iced-tea glass flanked on either side by mismatched water glasses.

I thank Michael for his help, but I make sure I get to the dishwasher first next time.

That's somewhat understandable though. After all, the kitchen is my domain.

What I don't get is when they misplace personal things like keys and wallets.

My husband, for instance, doesn't like putting his wallet in his pants pocket because he doesn't like to sit on it. Instead, he just throws his wallet in his briefcase when he goes to work.

But on the weekends, he doesn't use his briefcase. So any other possible receptacle is fair game: jacket pocket, sweat shirt pocket, a full grocery bag, my purse, the car, etc.

Then, when he's getting ready for work Monday morning, he can never find his wallet. Generally, I can help him locate it pretty quickly by just remembering what he was wearing over the weekend.

But recently even that didn't help.

We looked in every jacket, sweat shirt, and sweater he owned. No wallet. Then he scoured "his" room—the spare room—but still, no wallet.

He checked his car, my car, my purse, and his briefcase to no avail.

Finally, he decided that his wallet must have fallen out at the store or in a parking lot, or maybe even have been stolen. Thankfully, he only had a couple dollars in it, but the wallet also had our last remaining credit card that we were keeping for "emergency" purposes. So immediately Michael called and canceled it.

A few days later he was looking for his glasses.
Instead, he found his wallet—with credit card intact—in his briefcase where his glasses should have been.

*She watches over the affairs of her household.*

—*Proverbs 31:27*

# 6

# Calgon vs.
# Soap-on-a-Rope

He prefers steaming hot showers and soap-on-a-rope, while she likes to let Calgon bath salts "take her away" (for at least an hour).

Everyone needs to just "get away from it all" every now and then. That's why people take vacations to such exotic locales as Hawaii or the Greek Isles. Those who can't afford that luxurious a getaway "make do" with the California coast.

Then there's me.

My finances (and since I've been married—"our" finances) haven't allowed for a real vacation splurge in a long time. So I have to settle for the economy excursion.

Or as I prefer to think of it, the budget-bathtub plan.

My tub is my ticket to paradise.

All I need is a good book, some hot water, and Calgon bath salts to "take me away."

It's not the same for men.

Bubbles and bath oils just don't have quite the same effect. Instead, they prefer pounding, steaming showers and soap-on-a-rope. At least, *my* husband does. One of his favorite memories of our honeymoon (not the favorite, one of the favorites) is the double-headed shower in the bed-and-breakfast where we stayed on the northern California coast. For nearly twenty minutes each morning he surrendered to the ecstasy of dueling showers on his back and chest.

I enjoy showers, too, but I'd much rather settle in for a long evening's soak.

And I come prepared.

A cup of steaming hot tea with milk and sugar and Scottish shortbread on a flowery china plate is essential when I'm reading Rosamunde Pilcher or Maeve Binchy.

However, if I'm reading Mark Twain or Louisa May Alcott, I'll sometimes substitute a tall glass of milk and cookies.

But not Oreos. Dunking's just too difficult when you're in the tub. (Those little crumbs from the chocolate cookie outside have a real tendency to adhere to the skin, especially when there's bath oil in the water.)

It took my husband a little while to adjust to my bathing habits because, like most men, he's a shower-kind-of-guy.

We'd been married less than a month when one night I told Michael that I was going to "have a bath" (an English turn-of-phrase that I've held onto because I like the way it sounds. So much more elegant than "take" a bath).

Anyway, he was busy in the living room, so he just said "uh-huh" and continued with whatever he was doing. Almost an hour later, however, he called in to me, "Are you all right?"

"Yes, I'm just reading."

"Oh. Okay."

But after another hour had passed and still I hadn't surfaced, he knocked on the bathroom door, then poked his head in, concerned.

He found me in the empty tub. Buck naked and bone dry. Clutching my John Grisham.

"What are you *doing*?" he asked in disbelief.

"I'm trying to finish this. I'm on the last chapter."

"But there's no water in the tub!"

"I know," I said matter-of-factly. "It got cold, so I let it out."

"Wouldn't you be more comfortable in a chair or on the couch?" he suggested in that maddeningly male logical way.

"Not right now. I only have a couple more pages to go."

Michael loves to relate this story to friends and family, and even new Bible study members.

But I don't see what the big deal is. Haven't you ever been so mesmerized by a book that your surroundings become irrelevant and you can't put it down until you've finished?

However, there are some bathing times when I forget the book altogether. Instead, I light five or six candles, carefully lower myself into my bubbly sanctuary, and lie back in complete contentment while sipping a small glass of sparkling cider.

This also confused Michael. He came in to ask me a question but, seeing me in my sudsy state, got sidetracked. Later, I realized that for him it was just a case of simple arithmetic: wife+candles+no clothes=romance.

Men have such one-track minds. My math-challenged brain never even factored in that equation.

Then there was the time we went away for a relaxing weekend with another couple to a lovely "cabin" in the woods near Yosemite. We all felt the need for an escape from the busyness of our respective worlds. And this was definitely the place to do it. No TV, no radio, and a phone that wouldn't ring because no one knew where we were. Sheer heaven.

After we unpacked and visited for a while, someone suggested playing a game. Needing a little time to myself, I grabbed a book from one of the shelves lining the living room and sneaked into the bathroom with my faithful box of Calgon tucked under my arm.

After ten minutes of debating which game to play, one of our friends finally noticed I was missing. "Hey, where's Laura?"

"She's relaxing with her best friend," said Michael dryly before launching into his favorite bone-dry-reading-in-the-tub story.

It's not that I'm antisocial. Sometimes I just need to be enfolded in a good, long porcelain hug.

Unfortunately, there are times when I can't retreat to my cherished sanctuary.

My husband has this strange sleep disorder that took me a while to get used to. Once he goes to sleep, if he's awakened during the first half hour or so, he's up for the rest of the night. So although the tub is my preferred reading haunt, the bathroom is right next to our bedroom, and if I turn on the taps, he wakes up.

In that case, I usually head into the den and curl up in my favorite chair. However, one night we had a sleep-over guest who was up late watching TV in that same chair—leaving me with no quiet place to sit and read. Finally, after exhausting every other possibility, I headed for the only spot of solitude left in the house.

Once there, I looked down longingly at my beckoning bathtub but knew a crabby husband was too high a price to pay for a long, hot soak. Since I only planned to read for a few minutes, I took the only other seat in the room.

However, I hadn't counted on just how suspenseful Frank Peretti's latest novel would be.

Two hours later, when I finally shut my book and stood

up, it was like one of those Wisk ring-around-the-collar commercials.

Only it wasn't my collar that bore the ring.

*Of making many books there is no end, and much study
wearies the body.*

—*Ecclesiastes 12:12*

# _7_

# **Shut the Door**

(a misunderstanding behind closed doors)

All my life I've been a sucker for romance. I blubber like a baby whenever I see *West Side Story*. Especially the tragic ending when Maria cradles the dead Tony's head in her lap and lovingly whispers, "*Te adoro*, Anton," as the tears run down her face.

There goes half a box of Kleenex every time.

Another one of my favorite romantic movies is *The Parent Trap*.

In fact, it ranks right up there on the romantic meter with *Gone With the Wind* and *Casablanca*. Of course, that's partly because I saw it in the '60s as a prepubescent girl. I didn't just identify with Hayley Mills, I wanted to *be* Hayley Mills. With the famous English actor John Mills as her father, I just knew her home was always filled with movie stars. And she got to travel all over the world. Besides all that, she had a great English accent. (But if it were me, I never would have let those makeup people stick me with that goofy wig she had to wear!)

Anyway, I thought it was so romantic the way the double Hayley's parents in the movie (the sexy, rugged Brian Keith and the beautiful and sophisticated Maureen O'Hara) finally got back together after being divorced for so many years.

But for all that romance, there was one thing about the movie that always used to bug me. Near the end, when the mom and dad are eating dinner, Brian realizes he's still in love with ex-wife Maureen and starts to tell her. However, right in the middle of his incredibly romantic and endearing speech, she points out that he's gotten some stew on himself. He tells her he doesn't care, but she can't concentrate on what he's saying. All she focuses on is the stew. And she tells him to go and wash it off!

"What's the matter with you, woman?" I used to scream at the TV screen. "Don't you have any romance in your soul? This is a big romantic moment. Let this wonderful, sexy man sweep you off your feet."

Then I got married.

Many women have to contend with husbands who don't put the toilet seat down. I'm lucky. I don't have that problem because Michael grew up in a household with four women, so he was well-trained by the time I got him (although there was one time early in our marriage when I got up in the middle of the night to go to the bathroom and fell into the black hole of Calcutta).

(It never happened again.)

I wish I could say the same for his shut-the-door handicap.

We'll be watching *Jeopardy* together—our favorite TV show, especially when we beat the contestants—and during a commercial, my beloved decides he wants a snack. So he'll head to the kitchen where he'll forage through the fridge and rummage around in cupboards and drawers to get the necessary dishes and utensils he needs. When he returns, he usually brings in a mammoth bowl of popcorn or a gooey plate of his famous quickie nachos. After I lose final *Jeopardy*—I always bet the wrong amount ... another one of those math things—I take the dishes to the kitchen to clean up.

That's when I encounter the first evidence of Hurricane Michael's destruction.

Crack; I step on a tortilla chip. Crunch, crunch; I grind my way through a river of salt. Whoosh; I slip on a blob of butter on the floor. As I bend down to wipe up the flattened grease ball, I spot some shredded cheese that I hadn't noticed earlier because it blends in so well with the beautiful harvest-gold-and-yellow-flecked-pattern of our 1960s linoleum.

But that's not the worst of it.

As I straighten up, I bang my head on the open silverware drawer. Losing my Christian cool for just a moment, I let loose with some colorful expressions I learned in my Air Force days. Immediately repentant, I ask the Lord's forgiveness as I gently close the drawer.

That's when I notice the open cupboard door above. And the one next to it. And the one next to it. And the door to the microwave as well. Call me fastidious, but if there's one thing I can't stand, it's an open drawer or door. And my darling has left nearly half the doors and drawers in the kitchen gaping wide. By at least an inch.

This isn't a singular occurrence.

Without fail, every day when Michael gets ready for work, he never shuts his dresser drawers all the way. Sure, he pushes them in after he pulls out his socks and underwear, but never all the way. I don't get it. Just another inch or two and they'd be shut. How hard is that?

But by far the most difficult thing for me is an open closet door in the bedroom. When I'm lying in bed reading, I simply can't concentrate on my book when out of the cor-

ner of my eye I see a mishmash of shirts and pants, a hodge-
podge of sweaters tossed every which way, Mickey Mouse
suspenders peeping from inside a tux, and a jumble of shoes
on the floor.

I like—no, need—to see order and beauty around me.
And an open closet door is simply jarring to my senses. So
I usually get up and close it.

I discovered I can't concentrate on other things, either, when the closet door is open. One night, when Michael was in a particularly romantic mood, he began kiss-
ing my neck. Things were just beginning to heat up when
over his shoulder I suddenly noticed the open closet door.
"Just a minute," I said, leaping out of bed in a single
bound to shut it.

"Way to wreck a mood," Michael said wryly.

A few days later, it was my turn to be in an amorous
state of mind. So I put on some Sinatra, lit the beeswax
candles, and donned one of my Victoria's Secret bridal
shower gifts. Then I led my adorable husband into our bedroom where I began gently nuzzling his neck and whisper-
ing sweet nothings in his ear.

Remembering Natalie Wood's endearment in *West Side
Story*, yet recalling that she had said it to the *dead* Tony, I
chose a French translation instead. "*Je t'adore*" (pronounced
"zhuhtuhdoor"), I murmured to Michael in my huskiest
bedroom voice.

"Shut the door?" he asked in some confusion, glancing
at the closet door. "The door is shut."

To this day, "Shut the Door" in our house means "I Love
You."

*May your fountain be blessed, and may you rejoice in the wife of your youth. A loving doe, a graceful deer . . . may you ever be captivated by her love.*

—Proverbs 5:18–19

# 8

# I Like Liver Paté, He Likes SpaghettiOs (Cold!)

Dissecting the eating habits of the male and the female of the species.

The world is divided into two kinds of people. Those who love liver, and those who hate, loathe, abominate, and despise it. You won't find any in-betweens, not where liver is concerned.

I confess. I'm a liver lover. There's nothing quite like a little fried liver to give me that iron-high when I'm feeling a bit sluggish and draggy. I know, I know, I could just take iron pills, but they don't have the same flavorful zing as a panful of fried liver. Then there's always *paté de foie gras*, or as we call it in our family, chopped liver. Yum!

My husband, on the other hand, gags at the mere thought of eating internal organs. In fact, he won't even stay in the same house with me when I get one of my liver cravings. He insists that the smell invades every room.

This from the man who eats SpaghettiOs. Cold. Straight from the can.

Talk about disgusting.

Although liver crosses the gender line, many foods don't. At the risk of being politically incorrect, I assert that there are some clear-cut "guy" foods and "girl" foods.

Take those adorable bite-sized tea sandwiches without the crusts. Definitely a girl food.

Cold SpaghettiOs? No question. Guy food.

A 16-ounce hunk of T-Bone charred to the consistency

of shoe leather? Guy food, all the way (I prefer my sixteen-ounce T-Bone medium-rare).

Then there's your basic gourmet guy food: cut-up hot dogs in chili. Or, if he's feeling really adventurous, two kinds of Top Ramen mixed together. Or that favorite dinnertime delicacy: Cap'n Crunch cereal. And let's not forget the Sunday night staple: Hamburger Helper.

Teatime is where we really separate the boys from the girls.

Having lived in England for three years, I became addicted to "a cuppa" hot tea with milk and sugar. In fact, I go through withdrawals if I don't have milk for my tea. Naturally, it must be accompanied by dainty cucumber and cream cheese or watercress sandwiches without crusts, followed by delicate little tea cakes or mouth-watering English scones with jam and clotted cream (in a pinch, store-bought cookies also work).

Most men say that making little sandwiches work for a meal is not possible. And my best friend's husband won't even go so far as to put milk in his tea.

Barbarian.

Then there's my brother-in-law. His testosterone taste buds hanker for peanut butter on a regular basis. But he doesn't go for that childhood staple of peanut butter and jelly sandwiches. No, he opts for a peanut butter and mayonnaise combo. And he's not alone in this particular food fetish, either. When I was relating this disgusting sandwich phenomenon to our couples Bible study group, a few of the guys piped up: "What's wrong with that?"

Men can sure put together the strangest food groups.

Others would assert that it's not just the men. My husband thinks my mixture of tuna fish, sweet pickles, and Miracle Whip—never mayonnaise—is pretty horrendous. Hey, can I help it if I come from a Miracle Whip family? It's a Racine, Wisconsin, kind of thing. We also slathered Miracle Whip on white Wonder bread with a little fried Spam. But not these days. We're all too health-conscious for that.

Now we use Miracle Whip Light.

Actually, I only grow nostalgic for those halcyon Spam-filled days of childhood about once or twice a year. And when I do feel the need to satisfy this kinder-craving, I just make sure Michael's not around once that Spam hits the pan.

Most of the men I knew growing up in the Midwest were the strictly meat-and-potatoes kind of guys. With just one vegetable preference: salad. Made with iceberg lettuce, a couple tomatoes, and swimming in Kraft Thousand Island or Blue Cheese dressing.

Canned peas or green beans from the Jolly Green Giant were about the only other green vegetables allowed. But Dad even balked at that. Sure, he'd swallow the occasional green bean, but generally he stuck to his creamed corn and candied carrots. My mom would periodically try to slip in something exotic like zucchini, but my dad would have none of it.

Yay, Dad! When it came to vegetables, we were like two peas in a pod.

Except that I hate peas.

They're round and slippery and they squish in your mouth when you bite into them. Yuck! But even though Dad didn't eat peas very often, he joined forces with Mom on the importance of *my* eating them (must be a parent thing).

But I found ways to outsmart them. The first trick was stashing my peas under the rim of my plate. It worked like a charm until Mom cleared the table and discovered a perfect circle of peas where my plate had been. (Hey, give me a break. I was only five at the time.)

Next, I went the polite route: dabbing at my mouth with my napkin throughout dinner while surreptitiously spitting the dreaded little green balls into its papery folds. It took my mom a little longer to catch onto this one, but she was wise to me after the third time I eagerly volunteered to clear the table. She caught me green-handed trying to dispose of my soggy napkin in the kitchen trash.

In desperation, I finally took a cue from the family hamster and began storing the peas inside my cheeks. This worked until the night my mom squeezed my chubby little cheeks and out popped a plethora of peas.

My husband, the SpaghettiOs king, naturally loves peas—and all sorts of other healthy things.

Yet like the men of my Midwest childhood, he also gets quite a hankering for meat and potatoes every now and then.

His top two choices? Homemade pot roast with carrots, potatoes, and gobs of gravy. Or southern-fried chicken, mashed potatoes (skins and all), and white gravy.

He calls it his "comfort" food.

My comfort food is chocolate.

However, as much as I adore brownies with inch-thick fudgy frosting, warm chocolate pudding with the skin on top, and Snickers bars, there's still a special place in my heart that only liver can fill.

> *Eat anything sold in the meat market without raising*
> *questions of conscience.*
>
> —*1 Corinthians 10:25*

# 9

# His Junk, My Treasures

Also known as, "Love me, Love my stuff." Or how women learn to cope with GI Joe collections and Elvis paintings on black velvet. (That's what spare rooms are for.)

# His Junk, My Treasures

"You're not planning to hang that in here, are you?" I asked my husband as he prepared to affix a shelf full of his favorite Disney figures—plastic, no less—to a prominent position on the living-room wall.

Dopey and Goofy really didn't go too well with my Monet, I explained.

However, since I'd already nixed his *Terminator 2* poster and his box full of ceramic animals, he wasn't about to budge on Mickey.

Oh well, I guess I should consider myself lucky. At least he didn't insist on hanging a velvet Elvis in our living room flanked by an ancient wasp's nest.

Yes, a wasp's nest.

My friend Michelle's husband, Doug, had discovered the nest when he was a boy and patiently spent hours unearthing it from the dirt. All his hard work paid off because when he finally pulled it out, it was completely intact.

He was so proud of his archeological find that he hung it in his bedroom, where it stayed for years. When he moved out, he took his beloved nest with him—much to his mother's delight. All through college it hung in his living room.

When Michelle married him, it was a case of "Love me, love my nest."

Although she never quite grew to love his childhood treasure, she did tolerate it.

Until they moved. Then she was able to banish the nest to the spare room.

As for Elvis, Doug wasn't even a fan. He just loved the wonderful tackiness of "The King" on black velvet.

Elvis started in the living room, graduated to the dining room, and finally wound up in the garage. But recently, Michelle was happy to report that "Elvis has now left the building."

Other things don't leave quite as easily.

Remember the wagon wheel coffee table scene in the movie *When Harry Met Sally*? Every woman I know identified with that scene. Because every one of our husbands has a wagon wheel coffee table just waiting to occupy a place of honor in our home.

My best friend Lana's wagon wheel was sports trophies.

Lana and I have very similar tastes: antiques, teacups, china plates, roses, and lace. Her husband, a sports nut, doesn't.

His house, which Lana moved into, was your basic bachelor's pad—heavy on function, skimpy on form. However, his major concession to decorating was a shelf full of trophies housed in the entertainment center in the living room.

The chrome and brass clashed just a tad with Lana's floral china plates and silver picture frames.

Although her husband let her have free rein in the rest of the house, he was adamant about the trophies occupying a place of honor in the front room. However, after about a year of marriage and several compliments from friends on his wife's wonderful decorating ability, he grew less adamant.

The trophies moved into the spare room where they live to this day.

Still another friend's husband collects GI Joes!

But these are nothing like those little plastic action figures kids collect from the local drive-thru. Serious dollars are involved here. There are shows held in convention centers where men can pick up their favorite Joe along with various pieces of action equipment—tanks, bazookas, even a six-foot-long aircraft carrier.

Knowing how important his hobby is to her husband, my friend graciously acquiesced to his building a set of shelves to house his army of Joes.

Spare rooms are a wonderful thing.

Unfortunately, some things don't work in spare rooms.

Well-meaning moms send their sons off to college with such kitchen castoffs as aqua Melmac dishes from the '60s or '70s stoneware in earth tones.

Great functional stuff for a bachelor—even better because it's free.

The problem comes when a fiancée enters the picture with visions of pretty china patterns dancing in her head.

"Why would we want to spend money on more dishes when we've already got what we need?" he'll ask when she voices her china dreams. She takes solace in the fact that he only has place settings for four, and what if they entertain?

But he has a ready solution: "We can mix the Melmac with the stoneware."

When we got married, Michael didn't have much in the way of dishes or kitchen things, but he did have a major piece of furniture he was happy to contribute.

And it wasn't even ugly.

But it was Early American.

A nice, sturdy, maple dining-room table complete with eight chairs and two leaves. Michael was pretty proud of those leaves, too. They meant that we could have the entire family over for Thanksgiving—without having to set up card tables.

But what he didn't know was that by the time I was twelve, I'd vowed never to have any Early American maple furniture.

Because I grew up with it.

And I was tired of it. It wasn't only that my mom had it. It seemed everyone on her side of the family furnished their homes with it. And on my dad's side, too.

Everywhere we went, I was surrounded by the same maple furniture.

But my dream dining-room table was made of gleaming mahogany or cherry with graceful Queen Anne legs. Even a rustic dark oak would do.

But since an antique dining-room table and chairs is several years and many bills away for us, I've finally made peace with Michael's table.

I just keep it covered with a variety of pretty tablecloths, place mats, or runners.

All men bring a collection of special treasures to the marriage table.

One friend was surprised after she got married to discover that her husband owned some Star Wars action figures (and this was *before* they re-released the *Star Wars* saga to movie theaters).

"You're thirty-two years old!" she said.

What she didn't realize is that every man needs his toys. Whether it be Star Wars, GI Joe, or Mickey Mouse.

Although Mickey and his friends moved to the spare room when we bought our house, I have grown a bit more tolerant over the years.

Now I can even take plastic—in small doses.

That's why we have a Klingon Bird-of-Prey and a Borg ship on a bookcase in the den.

Right in front of Anna Karenina and Madame Bovary.

*Do not store up for yourselves treasures on earth.*

—*Matthew 6:19*

# 10

# Nightmare on Our Street

Or as many refer to it, "first-house frenzy."
"What do you mean we can't remodel that
ugly '60s kitchen and bathroom in one week?"

A few years into our marriage, something strange happened to me: a delayed nesting instinct kicked in, and suddenly I wanted to own our own home.

This from the woman who had lived in twenty-some rentals in ten years and had been known to pack up on a moment's notice and move clear across the country.

My spontaneous, adventuresome side was one of the things that attracted Michael to me in the first place. In fact, when we were dating, we both agreed that we didn't care if we ever owned a house. Who wanted to be tied down to a mortgage and the headache of home repairs?

Not us. Especially since we both loved to travel and dreamed of living in Europe.

But all of a sudden, there was something incredibly appealing to me about a sanctuary we could call our own where I could unleash my eager decorating talents. (No more apartment-issue chocolate brown carpeting and basic white walls for me. I yearned to go wild with wallpaper and pound as many nails into the wall as I wanted.)

It took Michael a little longer to get interested in home ownership. But after the third year in a row of getting zinged on taxes, he saw the practical aspects of buying and we started house hunting.

Fun city! Especially going through model homes and gleaning new decorating ideas. The only problem with brand-new homes, however, was that there was no backyard.

And someday, we wanted to own a dog, so a backyard was essential—as were three bedrooms, two baths, dining room, living room, and a two-car garage. We both agreed. Those were the "must-haves."

But then I fell head over heels for an adorable two-bedroom, one-bath, with a remodeled kitchen complete with built-in white corner cupboards displaying blue willow china (my pattern)!

"Honey, I love this," I exclaimed. "What a great kitchen!"

"But, dear, it's only two bedrooms."

"I know. But look at that kitchen."

"But, honey, there's no dining room."

"I know. But just *look* at that gorgeous kitchen."

"But, darling, there's only one bathroom."

"Okay, fine. But I want a kitchen like that."

We then proceeded to look at a succession of houses that never quite worked.

Every one either needed a new roof or other costly repairs, didn't have the space we needed, or, most important, I couldn't stand the kitchen.

The main problem was that in the area we were looking, most of the older homes had only one bathroom. Although there were just the two of us, we had already learned that two bathrooms were critical for the health and happiness of our marriage.

Finally, after vetoing the twenty-ninth listing our Realtor had shown us, we discovered a little gem on a quiet, tree-lined street in the neighborhood we loved.

The first thing that grabbed us was the wonderfully large and secluded backyard. The next were the three bedrooms, one and a half baths, dining room, living room, den, and an unexpected bonus: gorgeous hardwood floors.

And just about the ugliest kitchen I'd ever seen.

Harvest gold walls, bright yellow-and-orange flowered '60s wallpaper, pistachio-green-and-gray tile countertops, a chocolate brown sink—minus disposal—dirty-diaper brown cupboards (that some would call dark taupe, but I just call ugly), and thirty-year-old orange-and-avocado contact paper lining the shelves.

Topped off, or rather, bottomed off, by hideous harvest-gold-and-yellow flecked linoleum.

"Now, honey, just imagine the possibilities," Michael said in a cajoling tone as he threw a desperate look at our weary Realtor, concerned that I might nix this great find.

"This is a nice-sized kitchen," chimed in our Realtor-friend. "It has a lot of potential."

As I slowly surveyed the tribute to the '60s, I imagined gleaming white cupboards with brass knobs, warm butcher-block countertops, blue-and-white patterned wallpaper, a white porcelain double-sink with a brass gooseneck faucet, and a navy-and-white checkerboard floor.

I pictured myself in my Betty Crocker apron whipping up gorgeous gastronomic delights while chatting animatedly with our guests who were perched on matching blue-and-white stools.

"Okay," I said to their mutual relief. "But I cannot live in this house until the kitchen is completely remodeled. It would offend my aesthetic sensibilities too much."

Besides, between close of escrow and our move-in date, there were a spare three weeks. Plenty of time to remodel both the kitchen and the hall bathroom.

Oh, did I forget to mention that the same revolting pistachio-green-and-gray tile had been repeated in the bathroom as well? Only there it was offset by avocado walls and a dark beige tub, sink, and commode. There was absolutely no way I could enjoy my tub travels in that homely hideaway. So I added that to my remodeling list.

After all, I'd been down to our local Home Depot where I saw a nice, basic toilet for fifty dollars, a lovely pedestal sink for another fifty, and a combined tub and shower unit for just a couple hundred. By the time we added in sink and shower faucets and fixtures, I calculated that we could makeover the entire bathroom for under five hundred dollars.

And people say remodeling is expensive.

What it is, is time-consuming. I had no idea everything took so long.

Even such a simple task as pulling up old carpeting to get to the hardwood floor beneath became a week-long production. The actual pulling up of the carpet only took half an hour. It was the arduous task of pulling out heavy-duty carpet pad staples every inch or so that took so many man, woman, niece, and nephew hours.

Okay, so maybe it was a bit optimistic to expect an entire bath and kitchen to be remodeled in three weeks.

Instead, we're doing the kitchen in stages. And Stage 1 occurred about an hour after the Realtor officially presented us with our house key.

I immediately tore into that screaming orange-and-yellow kitchen wallpaper and gleefully ripped it to shreds. We didn't have time to rewallpaper then, so for the next two months the wall was whatever you call that brown paper-like covering beneath.

However, Christmas was coming, and we had bravely—and foolishly—invited both sides of the family over for a traditional Christmas dinner in our new home. The wall looked a little barren, so Christmas morning after Michael and I opened our gifts, we had the brilliant idea to recycle the wrapping paper.

Quickest and easiest wallpapering we've ever done. A little Santa here, Rudolph there, poinsettias around the edges, and some Christmas plaid in between.

Martha Stewart could learn a thing or two from me.

Yet even Martha's expectations are a little more realistic than most new-home novices.

Take our friends Bill and Andrea who bought a charming fixer-upper in one of the most beautiful old neighborhoods in town. They moved in early in the fall, and she thought her house would be picture-perfect by Christmas.

Well, the second Christmas came and went, and it was still far from perfect. Something about having to reroof, repair dry rot, gut the entire kitchen and bath, replace all the existing windows, rewire here and there, and paint everything.

Andrea and I possess a common bond that not too many friends share: an enthusiastic grip on unreality.

We plow merrily along with our idealistic fantasies, cheerfully ignoring gentle suggestions from our more practical husbands until we run headfirst into a brick wall.

My brick wall was Michael's wrists giving out—a scant three weeks into our remodeling frenzy. The doctor told him he had severe tendonitis and must wear wrist splints. Oh, and by the way, no manual labor for a month.

So much for my remodeling time line.

But probably the best thing for our marriage.

Somehow, the cozy picture I had of the two of us working blissfully side by side to transform our "cosmetic fixer-upper" into House Beautiful didn't quite work out the way I'd envisioned.

Instead, it quickly turned into a horror movie: *Nightmare on Our Street,* with each of us turning into monsters we didn't recognize.

Good thing God called an intermission.

While Michael relaxed with his popcorn and soda, I just took my trusty paintbrush to the kitchen walls and cupboards, hung a white eyelet curtain at the window, and put out as many blue-and-white pretties as possible to draw attention from the hated harvest-gold floor.

And when guests come over, I just tell them to look up.

*Unless the LORD builds the house, its builder labors in vain.*

—*Psalm 127:1*

# 11

# "Chick" Logic

(a.k.a. Laura-Logic in our household)
Although she received high marks in school,
she was absent the day they taught logic. For
instance, she thinks moving to Seattle would
be fun, but he says it rains too much. "So
we'll live in the suburbs!"

Men and women do not think the same. Or behave the same.

We're just different.

But that doesn't mean we all fit the standard male/female stereotypes. For example, in our marriage, I'm the one who channel surfs at the speed of light while my husband quilts.

When it comes down to how we perceive and respond to things, however, there is a Grand Canyon between the sexes.

When we were engaged and began discussing the big "M" word (money) in preparation for financing our wedding, Michael was taken aback to discover that I didn't balance my checkbook.

It wasn't that I hadn't tried, but I could never quite get the numbers to match up. And besides, it was so time-consuming and frustrating. Instead, I'd just look at the ending balance to see how much was left in my account, then go to the movies.

That was my husband's first encounter with "Laura-logic."

Then there was the time after we were married—yes, he still married me, but *he* balances the checkbook—when we were discussing whether we wanted to stay in California or move elsewhere.

I suggested Seattle. After all, it's renowned for its verdant beauty and terrific cultural attractions, and at the time was ranked the No. 1 desirable place to live in the U.S.

Michael, who suffers from that sun-deprivation-syndrome thing, said it was too dreary and rains too much to live in that city.

I replied, "So we'll live in the suburbs."

It's not that I'm stupid.

After all, I received high marks in most of my school subjects—except math—and even won a few scholarships to college. I think I was just absent the day they taught logic.

Or as my mother always says, "You're very smart in book-learning, you just don't have any common sense."

That's why in high school, the engine of my first car, a 1967 Volkswagen bug, seized up because I neglected to keep oil in it.

Gas. Oil. What's the difference? They're both liquids. When you run out, you put more in.

There's Laura-logic and there's "chick" logic.

When our friends Lana and Michael were landscaping their backyard, they worked together pouring the cement, laying the bricks, rolling out the sod, and planting the flowers. After all this hard work, Lana—my petite little fashion-plate friend with the beautifully manicured fingernails—was pretty sick and tired of all the dirt and drudgery.

As her husband relates it, when he later came in to tell Lana it was time to put up the fence, she looked up at him in surprise and said, "But I don't *like* fences."

"Chick" logic.

Then there was the time that the same Michael, a plumber, was discussing a potential bathroom remodeling project with my husband and me. We wanted to add a shower to our half bath off the guest room. The problem was, we needed to do it as economically as possible, and the bathroom's so tiny, there's not a lot of room to expand.

So I came up with the brilliant idea to just pull out the old sink, stick the shower in its stead, and place a lovely new pedestal sink around the corner in the bedroom like I'd seen so often in Europe.

"The difficulty comes in having to move pipes," Plumber Michael said. "That's a big job."

I didn't see how it could be that big of a job. When I looked under the sink, I only saw two little pipes on each side and the fatter drain pipe in the middle—totaling maybe two feet, tops.

How hard can it be to move two feet of pipe?

Laura-logic.

Recently, Lana tried to talk her Michael into the two of them joining a gym and selling his workout equipment in their garage, since he never used it.

He does use it, however. Every weekday at 4:30 A.M. while Lana sleeps on unaware, Michael gets up and pumps a little iron before getting ready for work.

But because she doesn't see it, it doesn't happen.

"Chick" logic.

My Michael says that another one of my illogical tendencies is that I think, therefore, I am.

He's referring to my being disorganized.

But I've always perceived myself as being very organized. A former secretary, I've arranged countless files in several offices into nice, orderly systems.

Therefore, I'm organized.

However, in my home "office" that doubles as the guest bedroom with the half bath (still minus a shower), I have several piles of projects in progress. Somewhere in the midst of one of those piles is a stack of file folders just waiting to be filled, labeled, and filed in one of my four filing cabinets.

I *want* to be organized, therefore I must be.

My directional impairment also plays a part in my Laura-logic (like north being whichever way I'm facing).

Or take, for instance, when we first got married and were going through that initially awkward "Which side of the bed do you sleep on?" I said that I'd always slept on the left side.

And I did. In our first apartment. Then we moved.

In our new bedroom, the bed was facing a different direction—I don't know if it was north or south, it was just different—and I immediately claimed my standard side.

The right side.

"Honey," Michael pointed out to me, "you're sleeping on the wrong side."

"No, I'm not. I always sleep on this side."

"No, darling. You always sleep on the left side."

"Nuh-uh. I always sleep on *this* side."

By this time, Michael figured out that it was a spatial thing, so he patiently told me to picture how the bed was set up in our last place and what side I slept on. Then, he had me imagine the bed set up in that same position in our new room.

"Oh, I'm sorry, honey, you're right," I apologized as I clambered over him to sleep on the left side.

But I had a terrible time getting to sleep that night. I just couldn't get comfortable on that side of the bed.

So the next night I tried the right side and slept like a baby.

It's not a question of left or right. It's a question of

which side is closest to the bathroom.

Laura-logic.

This logic extends to many other areas—even phobias.

Michael thought when he married me that I was this strong, independent, fearless woman. Which is why he was so shocked to discover my fear of frogs.

One night we were walking from the parking lot to our apartment, when suddenly something jumped out from the bushes and landed at our feet. I screamed in terror and dug my fingers into Michael's arm. "It's just a little frog—it won't hurt you," he said to me incredulously as the terrified amphibian quickly hopped away. "In fact, it's probably *more* scared of you," Michael continued in his logical, matter-of-fact way.

"I don't care," I whimpered, still shaking from the surprising encounter. "It scared me. They shouldn't jump out at people like that."

Michael finds my shark phobia a little more understandable. After all, unlike frogs, they have been known to bite.

Ever since I saw the movie *Jaws* as a teenager, I've been scared to death of some great white shark chomping off my legs as an appetizer. That's why I refused to go to the shark exhibit at Marine World in nearby Vallejo—a Plexiglas tunnel where people walk through and see sharks swimming above and on all sides of them.

"But, honey, they don't even have great whites there," Michael said patiently. "And besides, you're separated from the sharks by thick Plexiglas."

"Yes, I know," I said. "But my luck, the day I go into that tunnel, we'll have an earthquake, the Plexiglas will shatter, and the sharks will come after me and chomp me to pieces."

Laura-logic at its finest.

Yet I for one am glad God made men's and women's brains—and the rest of their bodies—different. Life's so much more interesting that way.

> *So God created man in his own image, in the image of God*
> *he created him; male and female he created them. God saw all*
> *that he had made, and it was very good.*
>
> —*Genesis 1:27, 31*

# 12

# I Want the Moon, but He Has to Hang It

She wants a new patio, but while he's laying the bricks, she's lying in the pool. (Often she comes up with the great home improvement ideas, but he gets stuck swinging the hammer.)

One of the things we learned from our remodeling venture is that I come up with the great home improvement ideas, but I expect Michael to execute them.

Quickly.

"Honey, we need to install these new light fixtures. And we really need them up before my parents come over for dinner Saturday."

Then I walk away, leaving Michael holding the screwdriver while I arrange my teacups on the dining room hutch.

It's not like I could help him with that boring electrical junk. Even Uncle Sam knew I was technically challenged, which is why I flew a typewriter in the Air Force, rather than a jet. I received high marks in administration and general knowledge on my military aptitude test, but only scored 40 in electronics and a dismal 15 out of 100 in mechanics.

Besides, Michael and I do things differently. He's very methodical and meticulous when he works on something and wants everything done just so. Whereas I'm in a hurry to get things done so I can appreciate the finished effect.

That's why we don't do many projects together.

We tried painting in tandem, but Michael told me my brush strokes were going the wrong way. I felt like "young grasshopper" in *The Karate Kid* as Michael-the-painting-master demonstrated the "right way" to move my brush. Since

I'm no insect-lover, I told him this "young grasshopper" would be happy to hop over to the TV to watch Regis and Kathie Lee instead. (When Michael read this portion, he laughed and said I mixed my movies together. "Young grass-hopper" was from the TV movie and series *Kung Fu*.")

Whatever.

Karate. Kung Fu. They're both martial arts that begin with a K.

Anyway, since painting was only one of about fifty items on Michael's to-do list, he graciously handed me the paint-brush and moved on to his next project.

I began his list when we first moved into our nearly fifty-year-old "cosmetic" fixer-upper. When I finished, the list was three pages long and Michael was a bit over-whelmed.

Maybe because in addition to such basics as replacing all locks, doorknobs, and electrical sockets; rewiring and in-stalling light fixtures; laying carpet; wallpapering and paint-ing, I included a few critical essentials. Like making window treatments, recovering lampshades, and reupholstering a couple chairs.

Naturally, I expected my husband to do all this because he's such a Renaissance man. Thanks to his theater back-ground, he can design and build just about anything (be-sides, he's much handier with a needle and thread than I am).

But Michael had his own agenda, including such prac-tical things as installing attic vents, running electricity to his workbench, repairing a backyard fence, and installing a drainage system for when it floods.

Practical stuff is so boring.

I was much more interested in the inside of the house

and making everything look pretty. And as I pointed out to Michael, window coverings were a must-have if we didn't want the neighbors to know us intimately before we'd been formally introduced. So while he whipped up some curtains on the sewing machine, I arranged all my beloved books.

And while he textured the hallway, I fanned my magazines.

Then while he installed the light fixture in the dining room, I went to the movies with a girlfriend.

It's not that I'm lazy. It's just that being a handywoman is not one of my gifts.

My girlfriends can relate.

Take my friend Pat (the one married to Ken, the do-it-yourself king).

She decided she wanted a Victorian gazebo in their backyard. So for weeks, she and Ken pored over magazines in search of the ultimate gazebo. Finally, they sent away for some plans for one they liked.

However, when the plans arrived, they weren't quite what they wanted. So Ken, the-dandy-designer-and-woodworker that he is, simply adapted them and began constructing his wife's dream gazebo.

And where was Pat while all the sawing and hammering was going on?

At the movies with me.

While we both have the vision to imagine all sorts of wonderful home improvements, we're not too good at the execution part of it. And I hate to admit, we just don't like it very much.

As Pat says, "I would rather scrub a toilet than paint."

Personally, I'd rather paint. But I scrub toilets, too. (Michael can't do everything.) Actually, I quite enjoy painting now. Granted, the finished product is not quite up to my husband's exacting standards, but it's one of the few things I can do around the house without hurting myself or the house too badly.

Then there's another friend of mine who moved to the country when she got married after having been a city-gal her whole life. An apartment dweller for the past several years, she told her husband she wanted to fill her brand-new backyard with African daisies.

What she didn't realize was that before her pretty little daisies could be planted, her husband had to Rototill a fourth of an acre. And the follow-up to that Rototilled ground? Weeks worth of weeding.

I've never been a yard person myself.

The first year we lived in our new home, I didn't do any work outside except sweep off the patio. Michael's the gardener in our family. I couldn't tell a pansy from a petunia. However, I do recognize roses. They're those gorgeous velvety blooms Michael gives me on our anniversary. In fact, when I used to take guests on a tour of the backyard, I'd proudly point out all the beautiful roses and "some green stuff" that Michael was growing.

The flowers worked their blooming magic on me, however. Now I'm on friendly terms with pansy, petunia, daisy, verbena, sweet William, and salvia. I even worked side by side with Michael for two whole days hacking through more than thirty years worth of ivy in our "secret jungle" that we're attempting to turn into a secret garden.

And I had the mosquito bites to show for it.

Michael came in with a couple of bites on his neck and hands, but my arms and legs were a mass of itching red welts (and he wonders why I don't do outdoors more often).

That's why he went back out alone to repair the sagging fence in that insect-infested jungle.

Besides, fences are a guy thing. Just ask my friend Lana. (See "Chick Logic" chapter.) Michael says that Lana's and Pat's husbands have it easy compared to him, though. Because in addition to fixing fences, building bookshelves, and installing anything electrical, I also expect Michael to make quilts for my family and friends.

Can I help it that he's so multitalented?

Anyway, that was just the first year of our marriage.

Everyone in my family—and most of my friends—have their quilts now.

Maybe the problem is that we wives have seen *It's a Wonderful Life* one too many times. Remember when Jimmy Stewart (George Bailey) escorted the lovely Donna Reed (Mary) home after the dance in the gym? George asked Mary what she wanted. Then he looked up at the moon and said, "Do you want the moon, Mary? I'll lasso it for you."

We all want our husbands to lasso the moon for us.

Or at least hang it—"a little to the left, dear."

> *Whatever you do, work at it with all your heart, as working for the Lord, not for [wo]men.*
>
> —*Colossians 3:23*

# 13

# The Nagging Gene

Many women possess it but don't realize it
until they're married. Although we all vowed
that we would never nag, it's hard
to fight genetics.

Many women possess a gene peculiar to most females but don't realize it until they're married.

The nagging gene.

I never knew I had this gene until I'd been married awhile. In fact, before I got married, I always found it embarrassing and humiliating to see a wife nagging her husband in public.

So I vowed to never, ever nag my husband.

And I rarely do.

In public.

But it's hard to fight genetics.

Sometimes it's as if I'm possessed by that little gene. It just comes in and takes over. "Honey, did you take out the trash? Honey, have you straightened up that stack of wood in the backyard yet? Honey, have you had a chance to take those boxes out to the garage?"

The problem is that we each have our own agendas. And they don't always match up (okay, virtually never).

For instance, when someone's coming over to visit, my agenda is to have the house looking as neat and clean as possible and to have refreshments on hand to offer our guests.

Michael's agenda is to finish a project he's working on in the garage.

Or when friends are coming over for dinner, my agenda

includes having an elegantly set table complete with sparkling crystal, fine china, and lighted candles to greet our
guests when they first walk in the door.

Michael's agenda includes playing with the dog.

It's not as if he didn't warn me.

He did. In fact, he promised me.

When we were engaged, Michael told me that the one
thing he hates more than anything is nagging. "I promise
you that the one way to make sure I don't do something is
to nag me about it," he said about a month before the wedding.

That's a promise he's never broken.

But I don't see it as nagging, I see it as reminding my
single-minded husband of things he otherwise forgets.

And one way to do that is to make up the old faithful
"honey-do" list.

That's what most of my girlfriends do—some every Saturday morning like clockwork. They either hand the list to
their husbands or post it on the refrigerator where he's sure
to see it.

I tried that, but the first list I gave Michael was so long
that he got overwhelmed by its sheer magnitude and popped
in a video instead.

I learned my lesson from that.

Now when I give him a multipage list, I highlight the
top-ten items I'd really like him to accomplish.

Next, I stick an asterisk by the top five things I really,
really need done.

Finally, I take my red felt pen and circle the one item
that I simply can't live without.

That way he's free to choose.

Nagging is not limited to household chores.

There's also nagging for something we want to buy. My friend Ken told me all about it.

"If my wife has her mind on something that she wants, the first thing she'll say is, 'Wouldn't it be nice if we went out and looked at this? Now, we don't have to get it, mind you, we'll just look at it.'"

So Ken agrees to go look at it.

"The next move is if I show the slightest bit of interest, it's a done deal the next day," he relates. "It goes from a 'maybe' to a done deal, and I have no idea what happened in between."

I have no idea what Ken's talking about.

But Michael does.

Ever since our wedding day I'd been longing to buy a couch. And I mentioned it to Michael a couple of times. After all, I was thirty-five years old and had never owned a store-bought couch of my own. I'd just gratefully made do with a succession of hand-me-downs from friends, relatives, and garage sales.

In fact, our first couch was a burnt-orange velvet loveseat, the cushions of which sank to the ground every time anyone sat in it. We tried to dress it up a bit with a makeshift slipcover, but it kept falling off whenever anyone sat down.

That's why I was ecstatic the night Michael told me he'd received a bonus at work and "maybe, just maybe," we could use it for a couch.

Unwittingly, he said to me, "We could start looking around and doing some comparison shopping, honey. But let's not be in too much of a hurry. We want to make sure we get something we really like that's also the best deal for our money."

The next afternoon, our brand-new couch was delivered.

But I wouldn't say I got that through nagging.

Just what is nagging, anyway?

I looked it up in the dictionary, and it said, "to annoy by constant scolding, complaining, or urging."

Gee, I never thought of myself as annoying. But I guess you could say I did a little bit of urging about a new couch.

Then I looked up "nag" in my *Roget's Super Thesaurus*.

Even worse.

As a noun, synonyms for "nag" include "old horse" or "faultfinder."

Who wants to be considered a horse, and an old one at that?

The synonyms for the verb "nag" aren't much better. Complain. Needle. Whine. Grouse. Henpeck. Scold. Carp. Berate.

I looked and looked, but couldn't find "to remind" anywhere under nagging.

Phooey.

However, recently, Michael came up with a solution that makes both of us happy. When there's something he needs to do, I just write it down on a little Post-It note and stick it on the bathroom mirror so he sees it in the morning.

That, he says, is reminding. Not nagging.

(Maybe that's because the paper's so small I can't give him a huge list.)

For the rest of you who might be pondering whether "to nag, or not to nag," I think one of my girlfriends has finally cracked the code: "The best way to get my husband to do something I want is not to ask him," she said.

> *Better to live on a corner of the roof than share a house*
> *with a quarrelsome wife.*
>
> —*Proverbs 25:24*

# 14

# The Testosterone Tango

She can two-step, chew bubble gum, rearrange the living-room furniture, and carry on a nonstop conversation all at the same time. But when he's dancing the tango, he's just doing the tango. It's gotta be a testosterone thing that makes men so single-task focused.

I can walk, chew bubble gum, rearrange the living-room furniture, and carry on a nonstop conversation all at the same
time. But when Michael's working on a project, he's just
working on that project and has difficulty being interrupted
for such trivial things as conversation.

It must be a testosterone thing that makes men so single-task focused.

For instance, occasionally when our friend Bill is working at his computer, his wife, Andrea, will come in to ask
him a question about something. That's when Bill gets a
little edgy. "She stands there and talks to me while I'm doing something," he complains.

Andrea says, "I'll interrupt him, and he'll just drop
everything and say, 'Fine. What is it that you want?' I'm just
asking a question," Andrea says, "and he gets mad."

Another time, Bill will stop his work at the computer
and say, "Obviously, this is not the best time to do this."
Then he'll turn to his wife and sweetly say, "Yes, dear, what
did you want?"

It's that condescending "Yes, dear" that drives us
through the roof.

Michael does the same thing.

He'll be reading or working a crossword puzzle or something, and I'll go in to ask him a question. He closes his book
with a loud snap or puts his pencil down and says, "Yes,

dear" as he gives me his undivided attention.

Well, I didn't want his undivided attention.

I just wanted my question answered.

If he asks *me* a question when I'm reading, I just answer the question and continue reading. Or as that song from *My Fair Lady* goes (with a little lyric swapping), "Why can't a man be more like a woman?"

Life would be a whole lot easier if our husbands just did things the same way that we do.

Take garbage, for example.

When the garbage pail under the kitchen sink gets full, I'll pull out the plastic bag to dump it. As the trash settles to the bottom, I see that there's now room for another foot of garbage to fit into the bag. Not wanting to be wasteful, I'll carry the bag through the entire house emptying every wastebasket in sight before closing it up and depositing it in the trash can in the garage.

Not Michael.

When he goes to throw something in the garbage and it falls out because the pail is full, he just pulls out the plastic bag, ties a twisty-thingamabob on it, goes into the garage, and drops the half-full bag into the trash.

My friend's husband is the same way. And as he explained it to me, I realized it was a testosterone thing.

"I'm in the kitchen, heating up some soup for lunch," he tells me. "I go to throw the soup can in the trash, and I can't because the trash is full. So I just pull out the bag and take it outside to the garbage can."

"My wife, however, when she sees me with garbage bag in hand, will ask, 'Oh, are you making a trash run?' "

"No, I'm not making a trash run," he says. "I couldn't care less about the rest of the trash. I'm hungry and I'm trying to make my lunch. The immediate thing is to get the trash out so I can eat."

Like I said, it's that single-task-focused testosterone thing.

I think it also has something to do with their powers of concentration.

As my friend Katie revealed, "When my husband turns on the TV, he intends to watch it, while I intend to use it as something to spark conversation."

She doesn't understand when her husband gets annoyed.

Rumor has it that some men are that way about watching football, too, but I'm delighted to say that I don't have any up-close-and-personal knowledge about this because my husband is not a big football fan. (Hallelujah!)

Men's single-task focus-ness also extends to the workplace.

For instance, one of our friends is a cameraman for a local news station—an exciting but all-consuming job. When he's working, he's completely focused on his work and his mind has no room for anything else.

Like social engagements.

So when his boss asks if he can work an extra shift on Saturday, he says, "Okay." Then when he gets home, his wife reminds him that Saturday is her parents' fiftieth wedding anniversary.

Most wives become the appointment secretary by default.

Take our cameraman friend. While he and his wife were dating, his bride-to-be bought him a nice appointment book so he could keep track of all his business and personal engagements. He thanked her for the very thoughtful gift and put it in his briefcase.

Five years later it's still in the briefcase without a single entry.

Now when his boss asks him if he can work an extra shift, he says, "I don't know. Let me check."

He calls his wife, the keeper-of-the-calendar, who says, "No, you're busy Saturday."

"What about Saturday night?"

"No. You're *very* busy Saturday night."

Some women become the appointment secretary even before they have their marriage license in hand.

There was an engaged couple in our Bible study whose wedding was just a few days away. As they were walking out the door, someone asked, "Will you be back in time for Bible study in two weeks?"

He said no. She said yes.

Simultaneously.

She turned to her fiancé and patiently said, "Honey, we get married on the twenty-eighth, we get back from our honeymoon on the fourth, we'll be in church on the fifth, and at Bible study on the ninth."

Single-task-focused as only a man can be, her bridegroom-to-be was thinking only of the honeymoon.

> *There is a time for everything, and a season for every activity under heaven.*
>
> —*Ecclesiastes 3:1*

# She's Felix, He's Oscar

When it comes to neatness, they're definitely
"The Odd Couple." (But let's not be sexist. In
some households, she's Oscar!)

When it comes to neatness, husbands and wives are often like Felix and Oscar in *The Odd Couple*.

But let's not be sexist. You don't have to be a man to be Oscar.

Take our friends Doug and Michelle.

He says he comes home from work and cleans up the hurricane every day.

It's not that Michelle's messy. She's just a stacker.

"Wherever there's a place to stack something, she sets it," says Doug, the minimalist. "She has piles everywhere."

It's the mail that really gets to him, though.

"I have separate mail baskets for each of us," he says. "When I come home, I go through the mail, open everything addressed to me, and take care of business before anything else."

When Michelle comes home, she just stacks the mail in her basket.

Doug says he's found unopened bank statements in there that are five months old.

But in Michelle's defense, she doesn't need the statements. Because she calls the bank daily and checks her balance through the automated help-me-find-my-balance-now system.

Mail is a bit of a problem in Bill and Andrea's household, too.

"Andrea will come home, open the phone bill, look at it, then set it down somewhere," says Bill. "The problem is, the place she puts it changes constantly. She'll say, 'This is where we're putting the bills.' A month later, she moves them to a different spot and says, 'Well, this is where we're putting the bills now.' "

Michael looked at me knowingly when Bill told us this.

I don't know why.

I only do that three or four times a year.

The problem for Michael and me is that we both brought a lot of baggage to the marriage. We each had several suit-cases of stuff crammed to overflowing in addition to truck-loads of boxes when we set up housekeeping.

My husband is quite the pack rat, you see.

He thinks I am, too, but he's wrong.

Okay, so I have a few thousand books. And every issue of my favorite magazines. And several hundred record al-bums.

Turntables will come back, you know.

To cut down on all this paraphernalia, when we moved to a bigger place, I suggested that perhaps Michael purge some of his stuff.

He told me to purge some of my books.

I was shocked that he could suggest such a sacrilege.

However, since Michael cleaned out a couple boxes of his things, I decided it was only fair to go through some of my paperbacks. So I weeded out a dozen or so mysteries that I'd already read a couple of times and dropped them off at our local used bookstore.

When I returned, I had a brown shopping bag full of books.

We both want an orderly home.

There's just never enough time to get it that way. But you'd never know it if you came to our house. The common areas are always immaculate (well, maybe not immaculate, but neat).

Something about hygiene, I guess.

Michael's quite hygienic. He's also quite hairy.

I'm not saying that he's furry, just that he and King Kong could be first cousins.

The difference is that Michael likes to keep himself well-groomed. And the maintenance for that well-groomed look includes trimming his beard and mustache regularly. Now, Michael is not a slob, but he only cleans up after himself when he's completely finished in the bathroom.

I discovered this after just a couple weeks of marriage. One morning when he was showering in our sole bathroom, I needed to brush my teeth, so I knocked and went in.

As I reached for my toothbrush, I shrieked.

The white porcelain sink was awash in a fine carpet of beard hair.

"Are you okay?" Michael yelled, sliding open the shower door in concern.

"Gross!" I said, wrinkling my nose in disgust. "The sink is covered with hair!"

Everyone has different standards of clean.

Like my mom and aunts for instance, who wouldn't know a dust bunny if it hopped right up to them.

My mom raised my sister Lisa and me the same house-cleaning way.

Except that all of our dust bunnies have names.

Which is why a recent Saturday morning found the three of us doing one of our favorite weekend activities: garage-saling.

Lisa found a used vacuum cleaner for only five dollars. But while she was waiting to pay for it, my mom said, "The only problem is that it's an upright without attachments. How will you be able to vacuum your couch?"

My sister and I just looked at each other.

"Vacuum the couch? *Who* vacuums their couch?"

Everyone, according to my mother.

I guess we both missed that little housekeeping have-to growing up.

Moms aren't the only ones who are so fastidious. One of my friends has nicknamed her mother-in-law the "Queen of Clean."

Yet neatness is not a gender-specific quality.

I know several bachelors who keep a very tidy home.

Like Felix Unger.

One thing that is pretty gender-specific, however, is the habit many men have of dropping not just their socks, and not just in the kitchen, but every other article of clothing imaginable all over the house.

My friend Pat said it was the one thing that made her crazy when she was a newlywed. Her husband would leave his shoes, socks, and shirts wherever he happened to take them off. That's why one day when he came home from work he found their apartment newly decorated.

Pat had quite artistically hung his socks over a chair, draped his shirt over a picture frame, and dangled his underwear from the dining room light fixture.

We women call that decorating with a point.

> *My people will live in peaceful dwelling places, in secure*
> *homes, in undisturbed places of rest.*
>
> —*Isaiah 32:18*

# 16

# Sub-Mission Impossible

I'm having a teensy-weensy problem with this submit stuff. After all, I'm the woman who kept a plaque on her desk in her B.C. (before Christ) days that proudly read: A WOMAN WITHOUT A MAN IS LIKE A FISH WITHOUT A BICYCLE.

Most couples have special pet names for each other—like Babe, Cutie-Pie, Honey-Bunny . . . and even more intimate terms of endearment.

My husband has his own adorable, sweet nicknames for me. Like Bulldozer. Speedboat. Tank Woman.

Not that I have a problem with control or anything. Or maybe just a teensy-weensy tendency to run down anyone or anything that gets in my way. Not really the most submissive of attitudes. Before I was married, I thought submission would be a piece of cake. In fact, I used to tell all my girlfriends, "I'll submit all over the place, if God will just bless me with a husband."

Little did I know.

Eight years later, I was married and asking my Thursday night women's Bible study for prayer on "this submit stuff." I guess I should have realized I might have a bit of a problem with the "S" word since for nearly twenty years I'd been a semi-militant feminist. In those days, I even kept a plaque on my desk that read: A WOMAN WITHOUT A MAN IS LIKE A FISH WITHOUT A BICYCLE.

My "feminism," or rather, independence, began as a little girl doing dishes in my grandmother's kitchen in Wisconsin. I HATED doing dishes. My sister and I were always stuck in the kitchen helping out with the holiday meal while the men sat in the living room drinking beer and watching football (not that I was interested in beer *or* football, I just didn't want to do the dishes).

Besides, my brothers got to play outside with their Matchbox cars in the dirt while we were banished to the kitchen. Personally, I much preferred dirt to dishwater.

But since I wasn't allowed to fulfill that fantasy, I retreated to my dream world of books instead. Most girls grew up on Nancy Drew, but Trixie Belden was my heroine of choice. I admired Trixie, the tomboy-sleuth, who along with her best friend, Honey, solved mysteries the local male adult authorities couldn't even begin to crack.

Movies were my other escape.

Early on, my dad introduced me to a world of intrigue and adventure where men *and* women traveled around the world doing daring and exciting things. I longed to be the graceful but wise-cracking Ginger Rogers in a diaphanous gown who danced her way into the heart of Fred Astaire, or Katharine Hepburn as the tomboy Jo in "Little Women," who headed off to New York for a writing career.

That's why I declared to my mother when I was about eight or nine: "I'm not going to get married until I'm old . . . at least thirty. First, I'm going to travel all over the world, have lots of adventures, meet interesting men, and become rich and famous."

I also said I'd have a maid so I wouldn't ever have to do dishes again.

Well, some of it came true, but I'm still waiting for the maid part to kick in.

By the time I was twenty-three, I'd discoed in Paris (it *was* the '70s after all); polkaed in Germany; skied—or rather, snowplowed—in the Swiss Alps; flown a glider over the English countryside, and drunk ouzo and smashed plates while yelling "Opa!" at a nightclub in Athens.

I'd also had my heart broken more times than I care to count, and I embarked on a course of self-destructive behavior that lasted until I was twenty-seven-going-on-sixty-seven.

That's when I met the Lord.

I still remember the first sermon I heard three days after becoming a Christian. The pastor preached on Ephesians 5:25: "Husbands, love your wives, just as Christ loved the church and gave himself up for her." As I heard the way Christ commanded men to treat their wives, I knew that's what I wanted and *had* wanted deep down for a very long time.

"Feminists are feminists because of men," the pastor went on to say. "Because some man has hurt them." I sat up straighter in my seat. How did he *know* that? Although it may not be true for all feminists, it was certainly true for *me.* It was as if the pastor had a front-row view into my heart and soul. Wow! If I hadn't been completely sold on this God-thing when I accepted Him three days earlier, I sure was now.

That very night, I went home and prayed for a husband. And my prayer was answered two days later (or so I thought). That's when I met a man at the church singles group who later became my fiancé. During our relationship, I did everything I thought a good Christian wife-in-training should do: I traded in my expensive silk dresses with the Green Bay Packers shoulder pads for soft and demure floral prints; began growing out my short, working woman's hairstyle for the long Rachel-and-Sarah look my fiancé preferred. I even started baking.

Talk about submission.

Whatever the man I was engaged to wanted me to do, I did. As a "baby" Christian, that's what I thought submission meant. But when my then-fiancé announced he was going to give me a sewing machine for a wedding present, I finally balked. (I'd hated sewing ever since seventh-grade Home-Ec, when I inadvertently stitched my sewing partner's finger to the polyester turquoise muu-muu I was making.)

"Why don't you get me a typewriter instead, since I want to be a writer?" I asked him. But he couldn't be dissuaded—it was critical that his wife sew. (Clearly, this was not a match made in heaven.) The Lord knew that, which is why He prevented that marriage from taking place.

Seven long, lonely years later, on my second date with a man named Michael, I declared: "I'm not giving up my writing for any man, and I refuse to sew."

He just looked at me calmly and said, "That's okay. I sew." (He also helps with the dishes.)

*That* one I married.

During our engagement, Michael told me he didn't want a wife who was a "doormat." In fact, it was my strength and independence that first attracted him to me.

However, those same traits—rearing their heads every now and then as selfishness and stubbornness—have also been the source of some friction in our marriage. As Michael gently points out to me, I tend to turn into a bulldozer or Sherman Tank plowing my way through anything, or anyone, who gets in the way of what I want *when* I want it (usually, "right now!").

Even though I'm incredibly blessed to be married to a sensitive, wonderful man who's not domineering, I still struggle(d) with the whole biblical submission thing. Yet, when I pouted about it at my study, made up of mostly single women, I was forcefully reminded of my single days when I, too, was wondering if I'd ever meet a nice Christian man who would love me the way Christ loved the church.

One of the women in the study had worked at the hospital where I'd been a cancer patient a couple years earlier. As I whined about "this submit stuff," she told the others of Michael's loving devotion to me during my chemotherapy treatments. Hearing someone else talk about the unconditional love my husband has always shown made me ashamed of my selfishness.

As soon as the study ended that night, I hurried home to plant kisses all over my beloved's face and to tell him what a great guy he was. "Wow," he said after I'd told him how terrific he was for the umpteenth time: "Keep going to that study!"

I did.

I also finally realized that Michael wasn't going to undergo some terrible transformation, take away my computer, and force me to be a "good, little Christian wife" by chaining me to a sewing machine for the rest of our marriage.

All along I'd fought submission because of a distorted view I had of what it meant. To me, submission equaled a mindless Stepford wife. (Remember that '70s movie in which the women were all turned into subservient robots through surgery?)

Yet I've never had a lobotomy *or* large breasts. Even after my mastectomy and reconstructive plastic surgery when I could have traded up, I didn't. (Something about that lopsided look.)

I *have* had a change of heart about submission though,

thanks to the Lord, an understanding husband, and the counsel of godly women.

"Your mission, Mrs. Walker, should you choose to accept it, is to submit to your husband."

I wish I could say that I always accept gracefully this "mission impossible" from God, but there are still times when it self-destructs in my face—due to my inherent need to take control.

However, all Michael has to do to get me to put the brakes on my overbearing behavior is say: "Just call me Bob, my little speedboat, 'cause I'm simply a buoy in your wake."

*Submit to one another out of reverence for Christ.*
—*Ephesians 5:21*

# 17

# I Say Exquisite, He Says Cool

## and other male/female vocabulary variations

While I was still single, a friend of mine became engaged to a very nice man who peppered his conversations with the word "cool." I remember thinking to myself, *I could never marry a man who said that all the time.*

Well, I did.

In fact, it's one of my husband's favorite expressions.

I'll tell him, "Honey, so-and-so just had a baby girl."

"Cool."

"I got a B on my algebra test!"

"Cool."

"I love you."

"Cool."

Actually, since Michael's not a laid-back surfer dude but an actor at heart, when he says the word he says it with enthusiasm.

"Darling, I just won a $100 bonus at work for a story idea."

"COOL!"

I appreciate the excitement in his tone, it's just his choice of words that leaves me chilled. I guess that's because I've had a love affair with the English language since the age of six, when I read 101 books in Miss Vopelinsky's first-grade class.

This love of words is just one of the many reasons I became a writer.

And I'm particularly fond of adjectives. Some of my best-loved are: lovely, elegant, breathtaking, brilliant, gorgeous, incredible, stunning, and last, but not least, exquisite.

"Laura, that's an exquisite dress you're wearing. Laura, your hair looks exquisite. Boy, what an exquisite teapot!"

Okay, so maybe I do say it a lot.

But Michael says "cool" a lot. In fact, early in our marriage after one too many "cools" I said to him, "Honey, you're a college graduate and a professional. Aren't there any other words you could use besides cool?"

He thought for a moment, then said, "exquisitely cool."

I wasn't always such an adjective snob.

But three years in England only increased my word sense and sensibilities. That's why when I hear words like "cool" or "groovy," it's like fingernails on chalkboard to me.

My English friends can relate.

For a while, I lived with a very well-bred Englishwoman outside the beautiful university town of Oxford. She told me of the time she took a culturally-deprived American GI to a London museum to teach him about art.

As they walked through the museum, she pointed out various works of art to the young soldier. When they came upon a marble bust of Mozart, the GI blurted out, "Mozart's neat." My refined English friend turned to him and said, "Mozart is many things, but 'neat' is not one of them."

However, over the years as I've gotten closer to God, I've learned how much He hates anything that smacks of pride and arrogance. And I realized that my vocabulary snobbishness could be taken as that, even though that wasn't my intent.

That's why I'm now much more accepting of others'

word choices. In fact, there are even some slang words that I've adopted as my own.

Like "coolness."

"Honey, I got a raise at work," Michael will tell me.

"Coolness."

Adjectives aren't the only words that cause problems between the sexes. There's a whole new language men need to learn when they get married.

Take our friends Mike and Jan.

He tells of the time late at night when he was dead-tired and just about to fall asleep.

All of a sudden, his wife, Jan, said, "I wonder what that noise is?"

"Probably just the wind," he mumbled sleepily.

A few minutes later, Jan, still wide-awake, said, "Hmmm, I wonder what that noise is?"

Mike grunted and buried his head a little deeper into the pillow.

Five minutes later, Jan said again, "Gosh, I really wonder what that noise could be?"

Comprehension finally dawned.

"Oh," Mike said. "You want me to get up and find out what that noise is."

My friend Lana's husband has also learned to interpret his wife's foreign language. For instance, he tells us that on the weekends she'll always ask him when they're going somewhere, "Do you want to drive?"

At first, he would answer, "I don't care. Do *you* want to drive?" But he finally figured out that if Lana really wanted to drive, she would. So now when Lana asks him if he wants to drive, she really means, "Would *you* please drive?"

"It's just another way of saying it rather than actually asking if I'll do it," he says.

I've always heard that after a time in marriage, husbands and wives begin to take on each other's characteristics, sometimes even begin to look like each other. Well, I have a long way to go before I grow a beard (but I must confess that in certain lights I can see the beginnings of a mustache on my upper lip. That's when I go running for the tweezers).

I have noticed, though, that Michael and I are beginning to use each other's expressions.

He says exquisite quite a bit now.

And it was clear to me that I'd climbed down off my lofty adjective pedestal when one morning a couple years into our marriage as we were discussing some house re-modeling projects, I turned to Michael in excitement and said, "Honey, you know what would be cooler than cool?"

*A word aptly spoken is like apples of gold*
*in settings of silver.*

—*Proverbs 25:11*

# 18

## She Wants It Special Delivery, Not FAXED

Although we like hearing the quick and basic "I Love You" from his lips, we also want sweet nothings sent "Special D."

"How beautiful you are, my darling! Oh, how beautiful! Your eyes behind your veil are doves. Your hair is like a flock of goats descending from Mount Gilead. Your teeth are like a flock of sheep just shorn" (Song of Songs 4:1–2).

We all wish our husbands would whisper sweet nothings like this into our ears—well, maybe not the part about the sheep and the goats, but we do long for them to speak paragraphs of poetic metaphor.

Instead, we get, "You look nice."

Not that "nice" is bad, it's just so generic. And impersonal.

Like a FAX.

While I want special delivery sentences.

Like: "Green is your color, honey. It really sets off your eyes and provides a striking contrast to your creamy alabaster skin." Or, "Your tumbling mass of riotous chestnut curls look beautiful against the rich ruby red of that exquisite silk blouse."

And the one that never fails: "Gee. That dress is really slimming."

Maybe I just read one too many romance novels growing up.

Since most men don't really talk like that, we wives would be happy to settle for one-word descriptions. Like ravishing. Sensational. Or drop-dead gorgeous. (Okay, so the

latter is two words—drop-dead being a compound modi-
fier—but gorgeous by itself just doesn't have quite the same
oomph.)

Just don't use the "nice" word.

Although, said in the right tone, it's not too shabby.

For instance, when we're going out somewhere special
and I've taken extra care with my hair and makeup, Michael
may say, "Wow. You look nice!"

That, I can handle. Especially with the "wow" preface.

I guess it's just that men aren't too verbal. Or as one of
my girlfriends said, "Women want more words in one day
than men have in their entire being."

That's because men tend to lean more toward that other
"V" word.

Visual.

Their eyes can appreciate how we look, but their appre-
ciation gets lost somewhere in their neuro-net before reach-
ing the vocal cords.

Instead, they use a soft touch or a gentle caress to acknowledge their regard.

And we think they're just after sex again.

We're looking for a little compliment, they're looking
for a little caressing.

Where we want words, they want action.

For instance, we'll be snuggling and Michael will tenderly tell me he loves me. And I'll dreamily say, "What is it
you love about me?" Or, "When did you first know you
loved me?"

I want details. He just wants to hold me and snuggle.

Maybe it's because Michael, like most men, is a very
tactile being.

He'll take a back rub over ten compliments any day.

Not me.

Just start piling on those pretty adjectives and I'm a happy girl.

Words just don't mean as much to Michael. Instead, he's a man of action.

And quite a romantic one at that.

I'll always remember how he wooed me when we were dating.

I was living alone in a cute little cottage behind a two-story house while I attended the nearby university to get my bachelor's degree.

Our first Valentine's Day together came just a few weeks after we'd started dating. That morning, as I was hurriedly walking out to my car to drive to my first class, I noticed something white wrapped around the car. *Great*, I thought. *Some kids T.P.'d my car during the night.*

As I got closer, I realized it wasn't toilet paper enveloping my car, but a thirty-foot banner that read *Happy Valentine's Day.*

That afternoon when I returned home from school, I discovered a small piece of masking tape with a red arrow attached to my front door. As I turned in the direction of the arrow, I noticed another piece of tape with yet another red arrow, which led me to still another piece of tape.

I followed this masking tape trail around to the utility room at the side of the cottage where I was greeted with a glorious bouquet of tulips. Eleven pink and one red.

And that wasn't all.

There was also a red heart-shaped tin filled with chocolates and an oversized just-right greeting card—not too mushy, but definitely from more than just a friend.

That's when I first started to fall for the guy.

Later that night when Michael came to pick me up for our date, I answered the door in gooey, romantic anticipation. Then I saw him standing on the front stoop in bright red pants, pale blue Oxford button-down shirt, and handmade red bow tie dotted with hearts.

Michael really goes all out for holidays.

But not in the traditional way.

Which is why he gave me tulips rather than roses that first Valentine's Day. But more important than just trying to be non-traditional, he remembered my saying that I really liked them.

I like daffodils, too. They remind me of England.

That's why a few years later he planted a whole bed of them for me in the front yard in anticipation of their blooming by February 14.

However, I don't always appreciate my sweetheart's creative thoughtfulness. Especially when I'm working in an office where the florist delivers a dozen red roses to every other woman's desk.

But I've learned my lesson.

Years ago, when I was a secretary in a high-powered office, one of the male executives realized on Valentine's Day that he'd neglected to get his wife anything. Knowing he'd be in big trouble when he got home, he pulled out one of his many credit cards and handed it to another secretary with instructions for her to select "something expensive" for his wife.

She returned with an elegant diamond necklace. And a mushy card for him to sign.

That was the same year Michael gave me a simple silver locket and a handmade card telling me how grateful he was to God for bringing us together.

The locket and the card mean more to me than the diamonds in a dozen necklaces.

And although Michael may not tell me that my hair is like a flock of goats, I'm learning to look beyond the words and appreciate what his eyes and his touch do tell me.

*You have stolen my heart with one glance of your eyes.*

—*Song of Songs 4:9*

# 19

# The Night He Saw Red

To him, the color red means "charge." To her,
it's just what she happened to wear to bed
(and other bedroom misunderstandings).

Most husbands suffer from an incurable brain disorder that their poor wives never find out about until the honeymoon.

Sex-on-the-mind.

Constantly.

It's a relentless disease that has plagued mankind for centuries. And there's no known cure. However, scientists have discovered a remedy to help keep this horrible male brain disorder in check.

Wives.

The only problem is, most wives are women. And their brains don't operate the same way as men's.

Nor do their libidos.

They're not supposed to. God didn't make them that way.

But since wives know they are the only hope for mankind, they're trying to do their part to help.

It's difficult though, because the slightest little visual thing can get a man to thinking about sex.

Like a red nightshirt, for instance.

My husband bought me a pretty ruby red satin nightshirt for my birthday one year that I absolutely loved. It was V-necked, high-cut on the sides, and buttoned down the front. But most important of all, it felt great against my skin.

He's such a thoughtful guy. With such good taste.

But what I didn't realize was that the nightgown was really for him.

That night, while Michael was in the bathroom brushing his teeth, I pulled on my pretty new nightshirt and crawled sleepily into bed. It had been a long, hard day, and I was exhausted and nearly asleep by the time he joined me.

However, the minute Michael spied that red satin, you'd have thought we were in a bull ring and I was the matador.

Charge!

Must be something about the color red.

Which surprised me. I always thought black was the preferred bedroom color of choice.

Evidently not.

Take some acquaintances of ours who have been married more than twenty years.

They're a sweet, conservative, rather mild-mannered couple.

Her color choices in clothes generally fall into the beige and taupe categories, with the occasional flash of navy blue thrown in.

That's why I was shocked when she revealed that she has a drawerful of silky lingerie all in the same color—fire-engine red. Or, as her husband slyly calls it, Frederick's-of-Hollywood red.

As far as he's concerned, red is the color of romance. And no other color will do.

However, his wife confided to me recently that when she put on an old red flannel nightgown and matching socks, it didn't have quite the same effect.

Other men couldn't care less about color.

Before going shopping for some pretty lingerie for a

friend's bridal shower, I consulted with her fiancé to find out his color preference.

"Just get something 'clear,' " he told me.

Clear? Transparent. See-through. See what I mean?

Sex-on-the-mind.

Which causes them to misinterpret even the most innocent of actions.

Like the times I slide into bed *au naturel*, simply because I like the feel of crisp, cool sheets against my bare skin.

To my husband, this is a clear-cut invitation to the dance.

The romance dance, that is.

And dancing is the farthest thing from my mind. Sleep is what I'm after.

But not always.

Sometimes I'm the one who begins the mating dance.

You know what I'm talking about, ladies. The one that involves candlelight, champagne, soft music, perfume, and your sexiest nightgown.

The only problem is, by the time I've finished with all this prep work, *he's* asleep.

And they say women never take the initiative.

I know of one California wife who for her husband's fortieth birthday, kidnapped him from a board meeting in progress and whisked him off to their favorite hotel in New Orleans.

That woman had class.

And money.

I can't afford to whisk Michael off to New Orleans, but I have been known to kidnap him and take him to a nearby bed-and-breakfast.

Right down the hall in our guest bedroom.

Creative courting is important in marriage.

I learned that in a Sunday sermon from my pastor. And since he's the father of eight, I think he knows what he's talking about.

He was encouraging husbands not to forego courting their wives just because they were now married. In fact, he said, marriage gives men the freedom to be even more imaginative in the romantic pursuit of their wives.

Like the couple who had a midnight picnic in their backyard, *sans* clothes. The only problem was when they tried to go back inside: the door was locked.

Romance is important, but it's also important not to get so caught up in the romantic mood of the moment that you forget necessary, practical things.

Like keys.

It's also important for us wives to acknowledge and accept the formidable responsibility we bear of keeping our husbands constant-sex-on-the-mind brain disorder in check.

And I for one am doing my part.

Except when I'm tired or have a headache.

> *Do not deprive each other except by mutual consent and*
> *for a time.*
>
> —*1 Corinthians 7:5*

# 20

## The In-Law Shuffle

You don't just marry each other, you also marry the in-laws. And to try to keep them happy, every year finds you dashing through the snow from house-to-house at Christmas.

When couples get married, they don't only gain a wife or a husband, they gain a whole new family.

The in-laws.

Which is not a bad thing.

Unless they take up permanent residence in your living room.

We're lucky. We've never had that problem.

Our "problem" is that we're both one of six children, and most of our families live in the same town.

Those first meetings with so many potential in-laws can be a bit daunting.

You know you're there on approval, and that you're being carefully scrutinized to see if you're good enough for their little darling.

Unless you happen to be my friend Katie.

When she was single, she used to accompany her married twin sister to all her husband's family's get-togethers. Years later, Katie met and married her sister's husband's brother. So when she married her husband, she knew more about her in-laws than she knew about him.

It doesn't work that way for the rest of us.

When Michael first took me to meet his sister Sheri, her husband, Jim, and their twelve-year-old twins, Kari and Jennie, I was a little nervous because I knew how much

Michael valued Sheri's opinion, and I was a little worried about not measuring up.

However, she made me feel right at home over a casual meal of potato salad, fresh fruit salad, and Jim's hamburgers hot off the grill. The best hamburgers in the world.

After dinner, while Michael was finding out what Sheri *really* thought of me—under the guise of helping with the dishes—Jim, the girls, and I joked around in the living room. We were telling funny stories when Jim slipped in a couple of side-splitting one-liners that set us all to laughing hysterically.

That's when it happened.

I snorted.

Then Kari snorted.

And pretty soon, we had a real snortfest going on.

Michael and Sheri came in to see what all the ruckus was about, and Sheri looked over at a surprised Michael—who'd never heard me snort before—and said, "She fits right in."

I told Michael later that I only snorted to get their approval.

He didn't have to snort to win my family's approval.

All he had to do was sing.

And my mom fell in love with him immediately.

My thirteen-year-old nephew, Josh, thought his new uncle-to-be was pretty cool, too. But it wasn't his singing that did it. It was his penchant for Mickey Mouse and roller coasters.

However, a couple weeks before the wedding, Josh and his mom (my sister, Lisa), were visiting me when Michael dropped by with a load of his theater costumes to put in the back room. As the three of us continued our conversation,

Michael suddenly popped into the living room in full clown regalia—complete with curly orange wig and red plastic nose.

Joshua looked over at me and said, "Are you sure you know what you're getting into, Aunt Laura?"

A scant two months later, Lisa and Josh both came over to raid Michael's costume trunk.

In-laws can be useful.

And fun.

It's just during the holidays when things can get a little tricky.

Especially when both sides of the family live nearby.

We call it the in-law shuffle.

Since "nearby" to some families means the same state, it gets a little insane when you live in a huge state like Texas or California.

That's because both sets of parents—and when there's been remarriages, multiple sets—all want to see their kids on Christmas Day.

We know of one couple who leaves Sacramento in the morning to make a one-and-a-half-hour drive to Modesto so they can have Christmas dinner with her family. Afterward, they drive another hour to Walnut Creek to see his mom and stepdad. And have Christmas dinner again. Finally, they make a two-hour trek to the gold-rush town of Auburn for their third Christmas dinner at his dad's.

That's about the time they're ready to change from their holiday best into their new Christmas sweat pants.

Only now they don't fit.

The problem Michael and I face is not one of distance but of etiquette.

Every year we go to his sister Sheri's for Christmas

brunch. It's an informal open-house affair where the whole family is invited to drop by sometime during the morning to eat and exchange gifts.

Pandemonium breaks out as each family arrives. And the wrapping paper flies.

My family's Christmas get-together is a little different.

Small talk and *hors d'oeuvres*. Dinner with fine china and silver goblets. Dessert and coffee.

Then we move into the living room to exchange gifts.

No mad scramble and frenzied tearing of packages here.

My family has a very neat and organized system for the opening of the presents. Each member of the family takes turns playing Santa by distributing a gift. Then we all patiently—or not so patiently—watch that one person open their gift.

All very civilized and proper.

Except for the year Michael came in carrying his plastic neon thirty-two-ounce, mondo-gulp soda container and set it down amid all the Christmas finery.

Before he even knew what hit him, I confiscated the plastic offender, transferred its contents to a water glass, and hid the thirty-two-ouncer under the sink.

Michael knew plastic would never be allowed at the dinner table, but he had no idea it wouldn't even be allowed through the front door.

He's not the only one who makes in-law *faux pas*.

There was the time I was trying to cheer up Michael's teenage niece who was a little dejected because she didn't have a boyfriend. I told her I didn't date much in high school, either, and that it takes a while to find Prince Charming: "I had to kiss a lot of frogs before I met my toad," I

Michael turned around and said "R-ribbit."
That's when the snorting began again.

*For this reason a man will leave his father and mother and*
*be united to his wife, and the two will become one flesh.*

—*Ephesians 5:31*

# 21

# Talk Marathons vs. the Sixty-Second Speech Sprint

She can sit and visit for hours with family and friends, but after too much sitting, he starts to fidget or fall asleep.

I can sit and visit for hours with family and friends and even strangers I meet on the street, but after too much visiting, Michael lapses into a catatonic state.

That's because I love to talk, while he loves to "do."

This verbal difference caused some problems when we were first married and my friends or family would invite us over for dinner. We'd all visit for a while when we first arrived, then sit down to dinner where we did a little more visiting. After dinner, we'd move to the living room for dessert and visit some more.

A pleasant, relaxing evening as far as I was concerned.

But since Michael's visitometer reaches its limit after about half an hour of conversation, somewhere in the middle of a marathon visit like this he'd either start squirming or fall asleep.

He's just not a visiting kind of guy.

Our friend Doug is the same way.

He says that ten minutes is about his maximum visiting time. Unless the conversation is something that's interesting to him (like movies). But he hates to sit and talk just for the sake of chatting.

I guess that's why they made the "Chatty Cathy" doll, rather than Chatty Chucky.

I for one love to chat. To me, it's fascinating to talk to all different kinds of people—which is one of the reasons I became a journalist. So I could talk to all these people, tell their stories, and, best of all, get paid for it.

But Michael, Doug, and many other husbands are just not visiting animals.

They're not big phone conversationalists, either. In fact, Michael absolutely hates to talk on the phone at home (maybe because he spends so much of his workday on the phone with customers).

Whereas I could talk on the phone for hours.

And have.

And do.

Michael learned this the hard way while we were dating.

He tried to call me one night at the little cottage I was renting before we got married and got a busy signal. So he tried again about fifteen minutes later.

Still busy. He waited about half an hour and tried again. *Beep, beep, beep.*

About another hour or so after that, I was still engrossed in my phone conversation with Lana (discussing my brand-new fiancé, of course) when I suddenly heard a scratching at the window screen. My heart stopped for a moment as I imagined some ax murderer trying to climb in through my bedroom window. But then I heard Michael say through the screen, "Laura, I've been trying to reach you for the past two hours."

Oops.

That's why when we got married he insisted we get Call Waiting. (Personally, I don't like it because I feel so rude when I'm in the middle of talking to someone and several other calls come in.) However, bottom-line-Michael said that people (including him) needed to be able to get through on the phone.

Guys are really big on the bottom line.

For instance, Doug says Michelle will ask him, "What do you want for dinner?" And he'll say, "I don't care."

Which means: he doesn't care.

Women have a different translation for those three words.

Ask our friend Bill.

When he asks his wife, Andrea, what she wants for dinner, she'll say, "I don't care."

So Bill will suggest, "Let's get pizza."

"I'd rather have Chinese."

Doug can relate.

"Michelle will ask me what I want for dinner, and I'll say, 'I don't know. I don't care.' And she'll say, 'I want *you* to pick dinner.'"

So Doug asks his wife to give him some choices.

Which she does. He'll then pick one, saying, "I want that."

His wife's response?

"Really?"

"Why doesn't she just tell me what she really wants?" Doug asks. "All I want is for her to tell me what she wants."

My husband nods in agreement: "Bottom line."

I hate that.

It's just not that simple. First, I need to talk through how I *feel* about pizza or Chinese food. Am I really in the mood? "Let's see . . . I just had pizza a couple days ago. Chinese sounds good. Although . . . so does Mexican.

Except that it always gives me heartburn.

The same holds true for movies.

We'll go out to rent a video, and before we leave the house, we've both sort of agreed on what we want to see.

Once we get to the video store, however, I notice another title that interests me. And then another. And I want to talk through every movie possibility with Michael and get his input before we make a decision.

Michael just wants to grab a video and go home and watch it before he falls asleep.

It's that "do" personality of his. He'd just rather "do" than talk.

Not all men are this way. In fact, some are great talkers.

Like used car salesmen. And therapists.

It's just that none of the women within my circle of acquaintances are married to any of them.

Our husbands are all more or less what I call the sixty-second speech sprinters.

You know the type.

When they come home after having lunch with an old friend they haven't seen in ages, we say, "What did you talk about?"

"Nothin' much."

"How's his wife?"

"Fine."

"And the kids?"

"Fine."

"Does he like his new job?"

"Yep."

"How did he look?"

"Fine."

It's times like these that my reporting background comes in handy. Because I know what probing questions to ask my monosyllabic husband. Yet even my girlfriends without a journalism degree have had to learn the not-so-subtle art of prying information from their chat-challenged husbands.

Visiting and personal information gathering just aren't their gifts.

That's why God gave them us—to run those talk marathons for them.

Sometimes, though, our husbands know they need to join in the race, if for no other reason than to make us happy.

They've just learned to carry the right equipment to make the run a little less grueling.

This is the reason that now whenever we go to dinner at a friend's house, Michael always makes sure he brings along a board game.

*Let us run with perseverance the race marked out for us.*

—*Hebrews 12:1*

## 22

# Hold Me, Touch Me, Listen to Me!

When a woman is pouring out her heart to her husband, she gets a little miffed when he glances at the TV to check out *Star Trek*.

When I'm pouring out my heart to Michael about something, I get a little miffed when he glances at the TV to check out *Star Trek: The Next Generation*.

Now, I like *Star Trek* as much as he does—particularly the tea-drinking, Shakespeare-quoting Captain Jean Luc Picard—but when I'm sharing my heart, I want my husband to pay more attention to me than to Captain Picard or Dr. Crusher (especially because unlike most male *Star Trek* aficionados, he prefers the captivating Dr. Beverly Crusher to the beautiful Betazoid Deanna Troi).

I'm not saying he's an insensitive clod.

If I came in with tears in my eyes or told him I was really upset about something, he'd turn off *Star Trek* in a warp second.

He's just not as inclined to hit the off button when I want to have a deep philosophical discussion about the meaning of life.

Or tell him about the great buy I got at Macy's that day.

I don't understand why he's not more receptive. After all, his show's almost over anyway.

It must be that single-task focused thing again.

My girlfriends know what I'm talking about.

They come home from work wanting to talk about the day's events, and their husbands barely even look up from the football game they're watching.

They insist that if it's something really important, they'll turn off the TV.

But what's important to her is not always what's important to him.

Like visiting her mother.

Or who's dating whom at work.

"Unless it's something serious going on, it's like asking 'How are you' to someone," said one husband. "You don't really expect an answer."

But when his wife came home and said, "I quit my job today," the TV went off in an instant.

Sometimes, Michael will simply press the mute button when I come in to talk for "just a minute." But twenty-five minutes later, I catch him stealing sideways glances at Counselor Troi and Dr. Crusher.

It's when he glances at his watch that I really get annoyed.

We'll be having a very important discussion—maybe about a misunderstanding we've had and I'm passionately re-explaining my side—when after an hour or so, he casually looks at his watch.

Or the clock on the VCR. Or a spider on the wall.

My girlfriends would never do that.

We can have an intense conversation for two or three hours and never once break eye contact. That's because we pour our whole being into sharing, relating, and listening to each other.

Our husbands' beings get bored.

And hungry.

Michael has been known to excuse himself right in the middle of one of my discourses to go get a snack.

Which makes me completely lose my place.

And frustrates me no end.

If he really loved me, he'd give me his complete, undivided attention and not worry about a little thing like hunger pangs.

Or sleep.

That was a big problem for us when we first got married.

We'd go to bed about 10:30 P.M., and I'd want to snuggle and talk for a little while.

He'd want to snuggle, too.

But by 1:00 A.M. he'd be snoring.

And when he came home from work the next day, he would be really tired and cranky while I'd be eager to talk some more.

Maybe that's because I was going to school at the time and didn't need to get up until 10:00, while Michael's alarm went off at 6:00.

That's why we finally agreed that 10:00 P.M. is sleep time, not talk time.

I'm also trying to learn to give Michael the *Reader's Digest Condensed* version of events since he's really not into the details. Those, I save for my girlfriends.

I've also discovered that if I keep important informational updates that I want to share with Michael to half-hour conversational increments, his eyeballs are less inclined to stray to the TV, his watch, or those spiders.

And, while he's watching *Star Trek*, I no longer engage him in conversation. I just snuggle up next to him with a cup of tea. Earl Grey. Hot. And enjoy the show.

> *Like a gold ring in a pig's snout is a beautiful woman who shows no discretion.*
>
> —*Proverbs 11:22*

# 23

# Women Need Other Women, Men Just Need Their Wives

The last male bonding thing he did was when he and his buddies went to see *Terminator 2* for his bachelor party . . . more than five years ago. He's content to simply "connect" with his wife, while she goes into withdrawal if she goes more than a week without relating to her women friends!

When I hear about male bonding, I wonder just who *are* these men?

And *where* are they?

My husband and most of my friends' husbands don't really bond with other guys. That's what their wives are for, they say. In fact, the last male bonding thing Michael did was when he and his buddies went to see *Terminator 2* for his bachelor party several years ago.

He's content to simply "connect" with me, while I go into withdrawal if I go more than a week without talking to my girlfriends.

And he's not alone.

Our friend Ken, who's coming up on his thirtieth year of marriage to the lovely Patricia, has always been this way. As he says, "My wife's my best friend. I'd rather spend time with her than anyone else."

So most of the time when he goes anywhere or does anything, it's with his wife (although he has been known to take in a *Star Trek* movie with one of his sons or another male Trekkie every now and then).

But that's just because Pat hates science fiction.

My stepdad's the same way. His male bonding is also limited to his sons. And since they're all grown now and don't live nearby, it's very limited.

Most men I know feel the same.

My husband certainly does.

He just doesn't feel the need to spend time "relating" with other men.

That's because he's missing the crucial "relationship chip" that God implants in all women at birth.

You know.

The one that makes less than a one-hour phone conversation with our closest girlfriends impossible. And the same one that enables us to discuss how we feel about nearly every aspect of our lives with one another.

This same relationship chip also allows us to "vent" to understanding girlfriends when family, friends, or co-workers make us crazy.

Not that we gossip, mind you (or at least try hard not to, being the incredibly spiritual women we are). We simply share our troubles with a sympathetic female ear.

It's a necessary thing.

Women need other women. Otherwise, our poor husbands would bear the brunt of our shifting moods and emotions all the time.

That's why my friend Katie even went so far as to have an 800-number phone line installed so she could talk to her twin sister on a regular basis.

And her husband doesn't mind in the least. He says it's cheaper than therapy.

God implanted a special chip in men at birth, too.

A stalwart, self-sufficient chip that eliminates the need for bonding with anyone other than their wives.

That's why Michael would rather spend time doing things with me than with anyone else.

Except when it comes to paintball wars.

Or Disneyland.

We tried Disneyland together once, but I just don't feel quite the same sense of wonder as he does about Uncle Walt's Magic Kingdom (of course, we went in January just a couple weeks after my final chemotherapy treatment, when it was cold and I was still bald and weak).

But even before chemo, my idea of a good time was not spending a full day and night at an amusement park.

Six hours, maybe. Tops.

Not my Disnoid husband.

He's there when those magic doors swing open first thing in the morning and doesn't leave until they click shut behind him at closing time.

That's why he was a little dismayed by my lack of enthusiasm and my suggestion that the management provide a warm place where people could just sit inside with a cup of tea and read.

"People don't read at Disneyland," he said incredulously.

That's also why the next time he went to "the happiest place on earth," he went with his old college friend Alan (a little male bonding by default).

Still other men enjoy sporting activities with their buddies. Like football. Basketball. Baseball.

Many women think the reason men enjoy these sports so much is that it gives them an opportunity to release their natural aggressive tendencies.

True.

But the real reason is there's not time to relate to one another when you're chasing a ball down a playing field. Or as one male friend so eloquently put it, "I feel the need to get with other guys so I can scratch and belch."

Let's face it. Men's and women's needs are different.

And that's a good thing.

Because while I'm off "relating" with my girlfriends, Michael's usually puttering around the house on some project or another—whittling away at that old to-do list.

Besides, if men only need one other person to bond with, I'm glad they picked the wife.

> *Husbands, love your wives, just as Christ loved the church and gave himself up for her.*
>
> *—Ephesians 5:25*

## 24.

# "And They Lived Happily Ever After. . . ."

The couple that laughs together
stays together.

I've been trying for the past couple hours to write this final chapter, but our dog, Gracie, won't let me.

The problem is it's early evening: kids are out riding their bicycles, couples are walking their dogs, and the calico cat across the street is slowly and insolently making its way back and forth across the grass.

Anyone—person or animal who comes too close to Gracie's home—is fair game for her frenzied barking and clawing at the window. I keep having to get up from my desk and soothe this savage "beast."

Understandably, Gracie sees these "intruders" as a threat to her "people"—Michael and me. And it's in her nature to want to protect us.

Gee, I feel an analogy coming on.

We want to protect the ones we love, too (like our spouses).

But even though we may want to, we can't always protect them from ourselves—especially when those Jekyll-Hyde differences are making us nuts.

Gracie never sees those differences, though. She just loves us unconditionally, whether we're preoccupied, grumpy, angry, sad, or just not having a very good day.

Hmmm, sounds like someone else we know.

But although we try to be like God, we often fail. In marriage, like any relationship, there are moments of bliss and moments of pain. Yet neither should define the boundaries of what constitutes a friendship.

So even though Michael hates my Spam, and I can't stomach his SpaghettiOs, when it comes down to the major life-changing stuff, our differences melt away and we are of one accord.

But you'll still never catch me eating peas.

> *Bear with each other and forgive whatever grievances*
> *you may have against one another. Forgive as the Lord forgave*
> *you. And over all these virtues put on love, which binds them*
> *all together in perfect unity.*
>
> —*Colossians 3:13–14*

For information on having Laura Jensen Walker speak at your event, please contact Speak Up Speaker Services toll free at (888) 870-7719 or e-mail Speakupinc@aol.com. To learn more about Laura, please visit her web site at www.laurajensenwalker.com. To write Laura, please e-mail her at Ljenwalk@aol.com or write to her at P.O. Box 601325, Sacramento, CA 95860.